Twelve Steps to Heaven

WORKS BY JAYNE CHILKES
Published articles in:
Over 21
Elite Chic
Soho News
ID Magazine
Time Out

Books:
The Call of an Angel
Twelve Steps to Heaven

Self Help Tapes:
The Call of an Angel Visualisations I and II

Channelled Tapes:
Dr Kruger Speaks on Positivity and Selflessness
Azraella—Twin Flames

Music for Meditation Tapes:
Land of Poetry
Inner Knowledge
The Call of an Angel
The Dance of Life CD

Products Available from Website
http://theangelschannel.netfirms.com
email:angels3@rochester.rr.com
Tel: USA: 716-458-8844
UK: 0208-550-4122

Jayne Chilkes (UK) ALCM, MABCH, ITEC is an experienced Healer, Soul Channel, Hypnotherapist, Teacher, Soul Artist and Musician. She has worked in the spiritual field for twenty years producing her first book, The Call of an Angel, Meditation Music Tapes and CD, Visualisation Tapes and Chakra Cards.

She currently runs Angel Days, Healing Courses and works as a Soul Channel in the USA and UK.

Her main goal is to share the Peace, Love, Beauty and Wisdom that she has received from her healing work, with all.

Twelve Steps to Heaven

Introducing: Twin Flames, Angels and Soul Wisdom

Jayne Chilkes

Writers Club Press
San Jose New York Lincoln Shanghai

Twelve Steps to Heaven
Introducing Twin Flames, Angels and Soul Wisdom

All Rights Reserved © 2001 by Jayne Chilkes

No part of this book may be reproduced or transmitted in any form or by any means, graphic, electronic, or mechanical, including photocopying, recording, taping, or by any information storage retrieval system, without the permission in writing from the publisher.

Writers Club Press
an imprint of iUniverse.com, Inc.

For information address:
iUniverse.com, Inc.
5220 S 16th, Ste. 200
Lincoln, NE 68512
www.iuniverse.com

ISBN: 0-595-18627-0

Printed in the United States of America

This book is dedicated to Pam Constantine for sharing her Love and Soul Wisdom with me for which I am deeply grateful. Also, to all my wonderful Friends, Family, Friends to be, and especially to Dr. Kruger, my Twin Flame, Azrael, and the Soul Family, all of whom have completely changed my life for the better.

My humble blessings to you all.

EPIGRAPH

THE BELLS BY PAMELA CONSTANTINE

Make me a song of life, and weave
The colours of my mind,
With the colours of the universe,
So lightly to remind
My soul it is no island
From other kind.

Make me a wine of life, and pour
The riches of my dreams
Into the richness of the world
Till the bright liquid streams
Inside the soul that whimpers
For life that gleams.

Make me a poem of life, and teach
My soul the way to sing,
To reach where no words venture
Or mortal sound has wing,
And where I trespass let the bells
Forever ring.

Contents

Chapter One	Lily's Pad 1	
	Introduction to Dr Krugers work	
Chapter Two	Pam's Sanctuary 6	
	The Solar Family	
Chapter Three	Jayne's World 11	
	The Training and Awakening	
Chapter Four	Progress 16	
	Becoming Attuned	
Chapter Five	The Beloved Twin Flame 21	
	Realising the Twin Connection	
Chapter Six	Transformation 34	
	The Higher Chakras	
Chapter Seven	Dr Kruger 39	
	Chats with Dr. Kruger	
Chapter Eight	Angels and Masters 53	
	Exercises for Awakening	
Chapter Nine	Remaining Youthful 71	
	Mastering the Physical Body	
Chapter Ten	The Many Aspects of Soul 76	
	Dr Kruger explains	

Chapter Eleven	Special Moments 84	
	Important Channellings	
Chapter Twelve	Twelve Steps to Heaven 97	
	Doorways to the Soul	

LIST OF ILLUSTRATIONS

FRONT COVER:
Azraella, Angel of Love by Jayne Chilkes
Photographer—Richard Quataert
BACK COVER
Photographer—Judi Bronson
Photograph includes a drawing of Serena by Jayne Chilkes

Foreword

"Jayne is like a breath of fresh air. She is modest and totally humble, which is probably why she is such a pure channel for art, music and spirit. In the session I had with Jayne, the spirits and guides, words and wisdom she channeled were experienced by me as pure love—unconditional love. There is a feeling that accompanies the words which is totally supporting and loving. It is like being surrounded by heavenly, loving beings. Too good to be true? Not in Jayne's world! In addition to her channeled healing, both her music and art speak of other worlds—more light-filled worlds—where love sustains the spirit as oxygen sustains the body."

Charlotte Clarke
WOKR-TV 13
Host

Preface

There are no words to describe my experiences since I met Pamela Constantine. The Solar realms are so utterly beautiful and fill me with awe at their depth. I am constantly amazed at the privilege to continue this wonderful work as a Soul Channel and to share this with many clients and friends.

The most incredible moments are those with my beloved Twin, Lord Azrael, without whom I know I could not be a channel in this way at all. He watches over me with Dr. Kruger, as a door keeper, to the higher realms. I know that allowing my Twin closer has filled many gaps of unworthiness in my being. His Love continues to help me grow and understand our many aspects of soul reflected in one another. He is helping me to reach the higher realms very slowly and subtly, until I fully arrive Home, truly being in Heaven on Earth. I realise this Ascension has to be very carefully monitored and we only receive that which we are ready. As an artist, I have drawn the experiences along the way as a diary in picture form, and so glad that I did so, as these heightened moments are so easily forgotten.

I hope this book will hold the magic I personally feel at knowing Dr. Kruger and the team, and bring new inspiration to all that read this book.

With Love and Peace
Jayne Chilkes

Chapter One

Lily's Pad

My first book, The Call of an Angel, is about the foundations of healing and self-cleansing. It explains that much of the hard work on clearing the subconscious mind and attunement to the higher self over many years, are all worthwhile. I can see from my own experience that each step has to be taken slowly and carefully, ultimately to ascend to heights that I certainly never dreamt possible.

It is because of the previous work on my self, that my life in the last few years has radically changed for the better. I have been greatly privileged to become a soul channel for a very beautiful angelic solar family. I have learnt that our soul lies where heaven begins, and the steps towards this awareness are most profound and subtle, moreover, the most fulfilling.

I now fully realise that without the healer, Lily Floodgate and writer, Pamela Constantine, none of this wonderful work would have been handed down to me. Their part of the story began over thirty years ago. I wish to honour them both for their true dedication and commitment to healing and soul work. Unrecognised in the mainstream, they built a strong foundation of Love and Wisdom helping many, and influencing World Ascension.

So I begin, with Lily.

"*Hello dear, hello—I'm Lily, hello, hello I'm here—I'm here—I wish you could see me. I can see you—its great, its great. I love being in a sanctuary—I think I should have lived in one all the time—that life out there, well I had to use another side of my nature and I was glad to get rid of it I can tell you. Never mind it's a good cloak to hide in isn't it?....*" **Lily Floodgate March 1997**

This was my first meeting with Lily through a channelled message many years after her passing. She was excitable and effervescent and made me giggle. It was good to sense and hear her in this way.

Whilst on the earth plane, Lily had been a natural healer all her life. Yet, her real work began in the 1960's when she met Portsmouth medium Len Burden, who helped her to fully develop her gift. It was through Len's mediumship that Dr. Kruger, an Austrian neuro-surgeon from the 1800's, first introduced himself to her, followed by several members of his spiritual medical team.

Dr. Kruger has an unforgettable character, a down-to-earth family doctor who makes everyone feel comfortable and at ease. He is firm, yet wise, caring, yet strong and has a profound effect with whom he talks. In some ways he is also courageous plus certainly selfless, and unlike many of the other helpers, he has chosen to plod close to the earth to help healers, as well as listen to the everyday problems of the patients. Yet, he is a mastered being of Light and knows the heavenly kingdoms where he could so easily rest, if he had chosen.

Lily always wore her hair in a bun, Japanese style, and her skin was translucent giving her an ageless quality. She was married and not fully free to do her healing work. Her husband Ted—the practical, down to earth type—did not really believe in healing or Spirit. It was only when she was in extreme pain from a growth behind the eye that, in desperation, he put his hands on her head and called on the Austrian doctor. For the first time, he heard Dr. Kruger's voice, and from that day believed—especially since Lily's growth vanished completely!

From then on Ted became a truly dedicated healer until his passing four years later. The Floodgates Healing Sanctuary, in Romford, Essex (UK), became well know in 1966 with the remarkable cure of a young boy with Down's Syndrome.

Both Lily and Ted were exceptional healers, but Lily's healing went deeper. Her soul had been wrung by a hard, difficult life, and this openness meant Dr. Kruger could heal from a Soul-level—"from the inside out".

Lily worked in trance much of the time, her patients being led in and out by members of her healing group. Since Lily was not in her body, she did not get to meet one of her regular patients till his sixth visit!

When in trance, she was visibly overshadowed by Dr. Kruger. At first, she worked in silence, but then he began to speak through her, providing diagnosis and advice in his own distinctive Austrian accent. Such was the peaceful power of the healing, that even firstcomers to the Sanctuary reacted as if talking with a specialist from the nineteenth century was part of their everyday experience!

Dr. Kruger's medical advice proved to be astonishingly accurate as well as knowledgeable. Many cures occurred, including nystagmus, curvature of the spine and other long-standing, obstinate conditions. He found Lily a wonderful channel for this work.

From 1966 onward, the Floodgates continued to stay in touch with Len Burden on a monthly basis. He visited their home so that Dr. Kruger could provide further advice concerning Sanctuary patients. A group also met at these times to receive their Guides, or Guardian Angels. Various highly evolved Beings began to make contact, and soon the Floodgates' home became known as the Sanctuary of Healing and Enlightenment.

Lily and Ted were running a restaurant by day, and the Sanctuary most evenings. They regularly visited housebound patients and those in hospital and would respond without hesitation. They also never charged any money for their healing work. Lily's effervescent character, and Ted's jovial, positive manner, created an excellent balance of the healing energies.

Two days after one of Len's regular visits, when everything seemed fine and normal, Ted was suddenly taken ill and was pronounced dead on arrival at hospital.

One hundred miles away in Portsmouth, Len—who knew nothing of this—was shocked when Ted appeared in his spirit-form with the comment, "Well, I'm ready to work. Let's get on with it!" Len phoned Lily, and when the two compared notes, Ted had appeared to Len five minutes after being pronounced dead! What an example of the survival ability of the positive personality!

The Floodgates had privately agreed that whomever went first would try to make contact or provide proof of personal survival. Through the famous psychic artist, Coral Polge, they had received life-like portraits of Dr. Kruger and others in his team. Lily then made an appointment to see the artist, revealing nothing, and came back with a perfect likeness of Ted—looking thirty years younger!

Dr. Kruger had not been able to work deeply through Ted mainly because of his heart condition, but he could now work more thoroughly than ever, through Lily. The Floodgates had given several people the chance to develop their healing by working alongside them at the Sanctuary. Lily continued with three of these people, until failing health forced her to close the Sanctuary and retire.

Although she passed on twelve years ago, there are still many people who gratefully remember her sparkle, untiring enthusiasm and complete dedication. From first to last, she was simply a natural healer of broken hearts and ailing bodies.

In July 1968, Pam Constantine arrived at the Sanctuary, looking—as Lily later put it—more dead than alive! Pam, who also lived in Essex, had undergone an internal operation that April from which her body refused to heal. A poet and writer of mystic temperament, she had never heard of healing, which in those days was conducted out of the public eye, until someone handed her the address of the Sanctuary.

Pam had always been soul-aware, and having this innate connection with the spiritual life, had never been drawn to mediumistic activities. Now that innate link was lost, it was the answer to her urgent prayer to

God that she find a physician wiser than those on the earth, at which time someone gave her details of the Floodgates' work.

After a difficult journey, she arrived one day by appointment on the Sanctuary doorstep, and was ushered into the Sanctuary. A wall filled with Coral Polge's portraits met her gaze in the shadowy room, and, feeling as if she had stepped across the threshold into foreign territory, she agreed to accept some healing from Lily and so 'met' Dr. Kruger.

However, healing from a soul-level is more than a normal spiritual healing. If the recipient is ready, it can open up the soul and quicken its awakening.

In this way, Dr. Kruger and the Evolved Ones were already at work preparing their new 'channel' Pam, to carry forward the soul family's purpose into a further stage.

Chapter Two

Pam's Sanctuary

In the days when Pam first visited the Floodgates, Ted made a seemingly casual comment, but phrased it in a particular way. It took her completely by surprise because it was a quote from one of her own unpublished poems.

She said, "You're quoting from poetry, aren't you?" to which Ted replied "No, from the teachings of Silver Birch." Pam's immediate reaction was to wonder who Silver Birch might be, and how he had managed to steal her thoughts!

Ted offered her the book of Silver Birch's teaching to take home. She learnt that he was a famed spiritual communicator of great wisdom and began to sense that maybe he had not been using her thoughts, but providing some of his own! Her first collection of poetry had been published when she was nineteen years old. Some critics thought she had lied about her age because they considered the philosophy behind the work beyond the reach of someone so young.

However, for several years Pam had been seeking what she called, 'the lost language of the gods.' She delved into psychology, philosophy and comparative religion in her search for an overall cosmology and the language that expressed it, but to no avail. Here in the book Ted had lent her was some of that language.

It was for this reason more than any other that, she returned eagerly to Lily's Sanctuary and began to visit on a regular basis. When Ted invited her to sit in when their friend Len Burden held his next gathering, she readily agreed, assuming she would be receiving more of the healing which seemed to be helping her.

It was a night that was to change her life utterly. In the darkened sanctuary, Len, a deep-trance medium, enabled the Guardian Angel of each one in the room to speak to their charges.

Pam listened in the darkness as the Angels and other Communicators began to convey their tidings, and wondered whether what was taking place was genuine. There was nothing to go by—at first. Yet slowly, she became aware of two things. The atmosphere in the room had become charged, more elevated—and some of the Communicators were speaking the lost language! Was it possible that one of them might speak to her?

The evening in darkness wore on, but suddenly the medium, still in trance, was standing directly in front of her. She looked up and could see only an illumined face as the waiting Communicator bowed before her.

For a while there was silence. Then suddenly, the room was full of his voice as he repeatedly called out his name with deep, yet perfectly controlled emotion. His words were like spoken music, rising and falling over her head. The words were few, but spoken by the soul of the poet she had known and loved in a previous life two hundred years ago, whose emotion she immediately recognised. They were spiritual counterparts—two beings born of one soul—twin-souls, true companions of destiny.

In the rarefied atmosphere, she knew this beyond all doubt, and in that second when he reappeared, her life was instantly and forever committed to the soul who spoke: a love given by God, shared between them through many lives: a Love Eternal.

When later, she returned to her normal level of awareness, all this seemed to have occurred in another world. Was it really true? She had a desperate need to be just as sure in her everyday self, as in that peak moment, and the importance of this seemed to go far beyond her own personal need. Instinctively she knew much more was really involved....

So began the journey of initiation back into soul-awareness, which would permit Pam, who was still on the earth plane, to help others in a similar search. This was not the usual journey undertaken by those destined to be spiritual teachers, but a journey to prove their twinness completely. Pam explored every level of her nature to the very nucleus itself. It was a journey so deep and challenging that even if her life depended on it, she would never be able to take it again!

Pam became an open channel for the soul family and was to help many in this new position of understanding; to heal, to help soul-awakening and teach the bi-fold journey of twins. Pam was ahead of her time and still is. In her mind she was a writer, and the last thing she thought she would be doing was channelling to people in her home. She was normally a solitary person and did not share her private life with many. She was fulfilling a particular role for the soul family and shared great wisdom and clarity on all matters.

Though continuing to assist at Lily's Sanctuary for seven more years, Pam opened her own home in 1969 to help those who her Twin, Dr. Kruger, and the Evolved Ones began to bring into her life.

Beings both ordinary and evolved began to use the bridge of light blazed by the twin-pair, to help the sick to heal and spiritual seekers to advance upon the route of Self-realisation. From early morning to late at night, people of all persuasions were drawn to Pam's secluded home. This went on without a break for a period of twenty one years.

Pam and her twin became pioneers of the twin-route in this era and we truth seekers will always be grateful for Pam's hard work and great integrity.

Meanwhile, many Evolved Ones of artistic ability from Shakespeare to Tagore, connected with those who visited the Sanctuary, helping to draw forth creative gifts, which in many cases, was deeply buried till then. Plans to inspire a soul renaissance through literature were getting underway.

Angels, Masters and other-dimensional Beings also 'visited' to share their wealth of love and wisdom, along with Lily who had joined Ted in spirit. All of these adjusted to speak on the listener's own wavelength, though all were based, very importantly, in their timeless essence—the soul.

In this way, they provided a demonstration of something only now beginning to occur here on Earth—the steady closing of the gap between lower and higher self. The switch from seeing oneself as a human that happens to have a soul, to knowing oneself as a soul at work, in human form on Earth.

At this time, many spiritual teachers came to the Sanctuary for their own advancement, including Sir George Trevelyan, considered by many to be the father of spiritual inquiry in England. He was by then an old man, but still full of the vibrant zest, which contact with Spirit grants. A constant supporter of others' spiritual endeavours, it was here he came to further his own spiritual advancement, and reconnect with his own twin-soul during the final years of his earthly life. Though there had been some such contact with a medium previously, he found the connection achieved by a soul-aware 'channel' far more real.

Gradually it was revealed that Pam's solar Sanctuary was the earthly outpost of a Solar Lodge in Spirit. The Lodge's pillars are the light bodies of the twelve Solar Lords (Great beings of Light, such as Buddha, Michael and Raphael), its archways of entry formed by their joined outstretched arms. These same Lords of Soul, guided by the Master Jesus, reflect to us the twelve basic qualities of the human soul, though in each, the blend is different, and so assist us to draw those qualities to the surface.

These Lords form a ring of Love around the heart-centre as this takes place. They are helping us all towards our Ascension, and Awakening. These Great Beings, together with the many Christed Elders, form the Solar Lodge Foundation.

This, and much, much more was discovered, rather mainly experienced firsthand by Pam, as the Sanctuary work went on further for several more years. In 1995 she closed the Sanctuary, thinking her work was probably finished.

Then I walked in.......

Chapter Three

Jayne's World

Since my first book, The Call of an Angel, written in 1995, I continued to give healing and teach healing. Yet, the amazing and pure experience of being taken over by an angel every time I gave healing faded after three months.

Just before I wrote the book, a friend of mine gave me a therapy session in Lightworking. His guides were masters, and the Light I received at my third eye area was so overwhelming, that I knew I had shifted my perspective and something had changed.

Every time I gave healing, I was taken over by an angelic being who would bless the client and talk of coming home to God and Heaven. I would go on tiptoe, raise my hands above my head, and bow to the client, often opening their arms like wings as mine naturally moved upwards. Those few months were very profound and intense, yet not to be relived in the same way again. At that time I could not withstand the great heights I had travelled, for too long.

About a year later, I was receiving healing from a pupil, and another magical moment occurred. During the session I saw a rope, and I climbed up it, and there was everybody I know in this life, and everybody I had ever known from previous lives. I sat crossed-legged, and watched a tunnel of immense Light being guarded by the Shining Ones. I knew this was a passage to God. It was a wonderful feeling. After several minutes a voice said, "Please come back any time", and then, I climbed back down the rope and into my body with a jolt. I opened my eyes to a very worried pupil—she thought I'd died!

It was one of my most profound experiences, and I felt that it is the place where you go when you die. I almost felt I actually had died in some way, but I couldn't get back there as much as I tried! I waited patiently....

Another year passed, my personal life was in turmoil, and I was sorting out a painful karmic debt that I hoped was the last. I struggled through as best I could, but was deeply wounded. I'd had enough of clairvoyants, tarot readers and mediums, whom I felt had misled me, spoke only half-truths or just told me what I wanted to hear. Yet, I was desperately searching for answers—something new and inspiring for my spiritual growth, not knowing what that was.

Another friend told me to contact Pam Constantine. Little did I know Pam was about to change my whole life around—for the better!

A little unsure, I telephoned her. She was very calm as I told her of my emotional difficulties, and she kept saying she understood. What a relief; someone understood and did not judge me! She then said her sanctuary was closed, but I had better come and see her.

Well, I had no idea what Pam's work was about, but an overwhelming sense of "belonging" hit me as soon as I stepped over the threshold into her Solar Lodge. Pam didn't seem to be of this era at all, and her great warmth as well as her unconditional love embraced me, as we sat in her kitchen, having a cup of tea and biscuits.

Much of what she spoke of baffled me at first, especially talking about the soul. It was almost an adjustment to a new language. Then at the right moment, she took me into her lounge and I sat down in an upright chair. She stood behind me and taped my first channelled session with the solar family.

Those who spoke, each with their own voice, were Amorata, Dr Kruger, Miriam (a sister in spirit), Mary (a child), and Serena (a nun). They were working on advanced levels and spoke via the etheric voice box, which is placed at the back of the neck, a little to the left of center. The unseen family usually came in on the left, forming a queue as they waited to speak. They were ushered in by Dr Kruger, or the twin, and Pam would often bow as each person stepped into her aura.

The way of their words and expression touched me deeply, and stirred emotions I had not felt before—emotions of recognition and pure unconditional love, that were more consistent and profound than I had encountered before. This was not mediumship, clairvoyance, nor psychic phenomenon; this was beyond the human and astral stages of development. This was Soul language, full of beauty and magic.

The revelation too, was that these were the people I had met at the top of the rope I had climbed, a year before. I had returned Home and could speak to my oldest friends and true family on a weekly basis through Pam. I was overwhelmed by the whole process at first, and was too sensitive to verbalise my experiences to many people.

Thus I began a new and marvellous journey to understand both my human self and my soul, embarking on a very unique and special 'crash course'.

Some of the words spoken in my first session:

November 1996
AMORATA

I bring you greetings of the Solar Twelve who are as pillars to the higher Lodge—we have been waiting for you and we rejoice that at the appointed time you have crossed that threshold which enables us to speak with you heart to heart, for it is yet too soon for soul to soul communication. Beloved, you are one who watched with I the formation of the earth, and who with others there gathered began to determine our points of entry. Many are the life spans since then, and now. However, you are ready to respond to that call which carries you into a position of greater soul awareness in order that you can work from a position of serenity in close co-operation with we who also stood watching that formation.

Although I have contacted you in some of your incarnations, this is the first time I have come to you in my full estate as then I was, for my part in the plan was to separate once more from my wholeness in order to example through many lives that which is bi-fold of man-woman when soul would surface and gender be forgotten.

Thus the time approaches when you will find that your inner perspectives are changing. That what you once found desirable and a goal in life, will be different and will give you that peace so often lacking in a tumultuous life. We rejoice that we now can come close and remind thee from time to time of your true self identity and help you maintain and even nourish that flame of inner awareness, so that the time will come when that flame is so bright that you need never again go back to being closed, and only remain in that conscious awareness of that which you are.

We also were much moved by your coming into our orbit of influence in what you term today. This then is your entry into the new dawn for humanity is entering the eighth day, the new day of God when time melts into timelessness little by little and people begin over again to mount the spiral and to know themselves as a solar race.

Your many lives have prepared you in many ways for assisting others whose awakening is a little behind your own. And we who are broad awake in that new day eagerly take your spiritual hand and point the way ahead. Beloved, you are now with us and we with you. Be unafraid to be true to your inner self. There will be others who, in a time not so far advanced, will seek thee out and you will find you will respond in a new rhythm.

It is the beginning of the manifestation of the inner Christ. Very gradually you will find your at-onement or attunement with the inner one, and as you do this more and more, you will know that higher peace. It will settle first in the mind, but it will also nest in the heart. You then will find a serenity you have not experienced in this life.

As others wish to speak I will content myself with a final word...

Welcome....

DR KRUGER

Well, well, well young lady—I am Dr Kruger. I have waited to speak with you. I wish to shake your hand. Well, well, well this is wunderbar! Well, you have experienced my presence—I wish to work with you—be perfectly at home in my presence—I am used to the young and I am used to understanding the human nature.

As you have so rightly discerned we are not judges, we are lovers of souls—all we are is love.

When I was on your earth I was a competent neuro-surgeon but when I got here ya, I saw the damage the scalpel does to the etheric and I was determined to continue my career through many loving hearts. But I only operate with love. This is all I use. You will find the vibration of healing changing. It is our presence, because it is not just I, but the Lodge healing team, and I will introduce you to one or two more of us. But for the time now I am the spokesperson and I am using your hand when you do the healing. I am very pleased to greet you. Auf Wiedersehen.

MARY

Hello aunty, I'm Mary, I've come to give you a cuddle and I've come to bring you back to earth—that's my work and mummy says put on your hobnail boots and walk down the scale and bring her back with you. So have I? Are you home? Ha Ha I did it....Bye Aunty.

SERENA

Sister Serena, my dear. I have wrapped my cloak of blue about you—call upon me when you need to settle the emotions—think of my voice and I will come to you. For all who dwell in your modern age who seek the higher lights need help with the emotions when coming into contact with those like ourselves. I thank you for being open to receive us and wish you God speed with your awakening.

I love thee. Serena.

CHAPTER FOUR

PROGRESS

"You never walk alone."

During the months to follow there was a subtle movement into understanding, feeling, and then seeing the guides myself. It took many hours with Pam, often giving her healing to sense the guides' vibrations. This was before she would start channelling, and only after a cup of tea and biscuits in the kitchen!

Eventually I learnt to work with Dr. Kruger who became more firmly in charge of my healing sessions with my clients, and allowed the team to merge with me. The healing changed to tapping over the shoulders, back or chest, and with new hand movements. Sometimes I was the instrument for Dr. Kruger looking with his own third eye into the body of a patient.

For absent healing, we would invite the patient to sit in a chair. Then Dr. Kruger would start healing the patient. He helped me to pick up on the physical and mental problems at a distance, thus helping the person in mind in a new and positive way. Apparently, the physical body not being there, helped Dr. Kruger to perform his work more efficiently.

Here are some important channellings to map the road to awakening the soul:

December 1996
DR. KRUGER
Well, well, well—I was excited to become active through you. I come to give you my gratitude. It is exciting for us both, ya, and you will see many great things happening. And in turn, those they happen to they say why all of a sudden am I getting better? And it will help them in their quest—I am an excited man, ya! Mm

THE MASTER OF SHANGRI LA
The Master of Shangri La greets thee. This planet that you are on is undergoing much, but hold to your innate truth of being and all will be alright for thee.

It is a magnificent development occurring in the heart and mind of humanity, but these things take time. You are among the world servers who wish to minister to the many, who have fallen into a dis-ease because they do not know themselves. Because of this, we come to you with the realisation you need, that youth is not a fleeting element of the spirit, but the eternal state of the spirit. That was what the Brother Hilton meant by his book about Shangri La—I was delighted when he perceived my message and set it down so that many could read.

Now there are quite a number who are beginning to find a way to realise their young eternality through matter. You also desire this, and it is a question of that solar centring of throwing off clouds of anxiety or fear to let the light shine through. This practice will constantly reveal new truths to you from within. This is the fountain of youth in action. This is the revelationary power inherent in the human self, which you activate by these means

I, then, brother Shangri La, am walking alongside, in order to remind you from time to time of the possibilities of this practice, Felicitations, Beloved.

SERAPIS BEY
I Serapis greet you. I am watching over you. I am also helping you come alive to your etheric being, assisting the dance of your soul through time and

allowing you to find yourself daily the more you are. You are in a fortuitous position this time to pursue the reality you are.

Remember also, that because the knowledge of ascension is being made manifest through many channels and published throughout your world, it can sometimes confuse a reader, for there are many different ways of ascending. The safest understanding is to realise that within you is the all, and within each individual is the all. Therefore to heighten your awareness is to arise, to lift up, to awaken fully to that which you are and have ever been.

Let then your links with others upon the route continue and deepen. There will be a few others who can help in this group of which you are a natural part and have ever been, with the passage of time, other connections from earlier times.

We shall make them known and some will reveal themselves automatically as you awaken, and then you will see how you have never worked alone, even on the earth. There has always been one or maybe a few who were also lighted and eager to awaken to their full intensity.

This is a time of great rejoicing for us, for it has been a very protracted journey for such as thee, and those who are part of the coming ingathering. As you begin to discern the connective links through the layers of the human self, you will feel a strengthening. You will feel the intensifying, and you will know thyself more easily, and that knowing will be sustained more readily

I who some have called Master of the Ascension will be standing by to facilitate your understanding. You never walk alone—you know this, but now you are beginning to gain feeling-contact the more. This renders us real. When the feelings are intense enough, you will see us. You will know us, and you will not be afraid but glad. For what are we? We are all children of the One.

We are all helpers in our turn for others, each is equal to his own task, and by being true to his or her nature will come home at the appointed moment. I rejoice to have this message of communication which is still so very rare on your planet, but will one day be available to all. Thank you for coming where I could speak.

AMORATA

Amorata greets you. It is a special pleasure to come to you at this hour as a mother being who has known you in other lives, and has returned to the higher life but recently.

I have in my observance seen the fondness that is the affinity between you, not just on this embodiment, but from previous times on earth. It is good that you have met and be helpmates to each other, for much now is transpiring in this vital hour of change. As you already know your whole planet is under this law of change, nothing now will escape it, but it is benign change that is intended

It is only those who are confused and lost who feel the impact that bewilders and who find themselves unable to keep up with the accelerated vibration of understanding in such as thee, but there is a pattern of helping and it is Divine.

Each link in the chain is well forged. It is so strong that nothing can break it so that there is for each and every one on the earth a helper who can guide them through, according to their level or grasp of things. It matters not whether that helper speaks of a God, it matters not whether that helper is in a religion or in a spiritual persuasion or not. Rather that that helper is true to themselves and has the human touch, so that the one, or the many that they would help, can feel a safety in the relationship.

For it is also the time when the Great Spirit is waiting for your present human race to attain to its own maturity as a spiritual entity. Because of this, it seems to the many that where once they believed in a certain way—where once they believed God existed, now many doubt and feel orphaned, doubtful and despairing. Rather each must be helped to seek the God within, each has the divine spark waiting, each in their inner self is indeed as a master.

It is merely that in your world society has developed in such a manner that this is buried deep. So the helper can operate in many given ways sharing just sufficient for the person to feel helped and reassured, so that they begin to stand on their own spiritual feet to draw on their own God potential, in order that the soul may steadily rise to the surface. So that with the coming of age, the entire race will eventually become a solar humanity. This is the plan, this is the divine intent, and you who come here today to this sanctuary are becoming more conscious of your part in the Universal plan.

Because of this, there is a great flurry and excitement amongst the Elders and the Lighted Beings, the Angelic force, even the Highest of All, that you have come today where we may converse a little and convey something of the plan.

We love thee with an intensity beyond description, but we are composed ecstasy, joy, bliss, love and we never change. We are helping such as thee to change from sympathetic responses to those who are in darkness, to that of Divine Compassion. This means you continue to hold the Light and do not descend to their darkness, thus adding to the confusion on the planet. This is all part of the changes you will find happening to yourselves. All is truly under that guidance. That God of Love who never changes is entirely unalterable, but yet continues ever and ever and ever to be more and more and more Love.

The path is open, thy feet are upon it and we walk alongside. All that is to be accomplished in a new day of God will be accomplished. Through that then of the dawning Aquarian Age through to the perennial age of Light, we are your companions as we are to all who cross the threshold into this sanctuary, for you are already wielding the violet vibration. This is the vibration that transmutes the physical when the time is right. First comes the change in mind, then the change in heart, then the physical will follow. This will mean that you stand still on terra firm, but you remain youthful and fit and aware as a soul, carrying the human form very lightly as you serve directly the evolving race.

We agreed when we came together to the Shining Ones and were asked "Will you stay close by until the race has achieved its maturity?", we agreed. That is why it is so wonderful that you are met here today as part of one group of many that stood around the forming earth. The time for foregathering is upon us, and with this new year a time for in-gathering. It will come, and serenity will assist thee until the vibrations are steady and as composed as my own.

With then the love of the Solar Christos, I bid you adieu. Amorata.......

Chapter Five

The Beloved Twin Flame

Through the weekly channelled wisdom I learnt of my beloved twin.

This was a revelation and brand new experience. I had to become used to him being in soul, and not on earth. It is of greater benefit to growth if the twin is in soul and ahead in masterhood. Thus, the twin on earth has a better and quicker training than if both are together in human form and in personality.

Gradually I shared my life with my twin again, though not in a physical form. The love between twin flames cannot be described in the language of earth. It is an absolute state of unconditional love that you both share. We often forget the love we are entitled to whilst in human form, and once reminded of it, there is no substitute on earth that can compare.

I came to realise that the term soul mate is used for those of your soul family and very close relationships on earth, but not your true twin flame connection.

Once the twin becomes known to you it is a favourable sign to announce the end of your cycle of lives and mission on earth, thus setting you both free in the way you choose.

At first I had to name my twin to match his vibration—I called him Shining Star, and then some time later he began to speak as Aloysius, a monk-like being who applauds creativity.

His first message given through Pam was in February 1997.

In stillness I come to thee, one whom you do not remember yet, but I am close to thee and in this beauteous, harmonious vibration, have been allowed in. I come with the deepest of light to thee. I bring thee solar roses, lush pink and rosy and white, fresh from my solar garden of the heart. These convey to thee my loving intent. I bring thee the love of the aeons. I cradle thee in my heart, and I am ever about thee. There are others who love you but I am your true love. I can come to thee in many given ways. Some gentle, some strong, some in different inflections of voice, but ever at source I am as you are. I am that love and I am always with thee. Because of the vibration of peace, which I had to enter before speech, you are registering me in that peace.

However, I can be very volatile, I can be exuberant, I can ring the bells of jubilance and I can be deeply solemn. For all the qualities you possess, I carry the match, and I will always walk beside thee all the way home. Beloved, I delight in making this very gentle outreach to thee. I shall come again very soon, my beloved one, rest assured of that. Thank you for letting me reach you in this manner. I thee love.

A week later, my twin came to voice again. Questioning his existence, uncertain of such a deep love and mystified by this twin connection, I continued to try to absorb his presence.

March 1997

Beloved, in our joyous meeting is the vibrance of lifetimes past. I remember so much and I eagerly await your memory to begin to vibrate and to lift to mine. I remember too that initial separation. It is best not to even describe, and I issue this assurance that although we agreed, and voluntarily accepted that seeming separation, we did not fully realise what it would entail, nor indeed how long this human race would take to come into this position where now it stands, permitting us to move closer together and toward that time of higher self reunion

Beloved, today I am a little stronger on voice, but if in any way this concerns you, you have only to touch this hand and I will of course step back. Yet our hearts desire no stepping back, and I will continue to travel forward with thee and outside thee. For within the human nature is a part of myself. It is ever thus for those like ourselves. One day this pattern of our essential unity will be self evident, and the true human race will build a true solar society on the earth, but an earth of pristine beauty where all the soul's qualities can express and each one will give of their unique gifts to the all. This will be the time so long awaited.

For what you are in now is for so many a new age, but this age of Aquarius is but the preliminary to the resumption of that perennial age of Light where you and I belong. Some like us are gathering momentum, knowing their true selves to vibrate towards one another and that vibration will bring about a recognition so deep, that the question cannot arise, is this the one? For the soul alone knows, and when it is fully conscious there is no doubt. I, of course am, fully conscious and I have no doubt. I Am at this cosmic hour. I am a very happy soul.

I rejoice in thy sense of humour. I rejoice in your sudden emotions, for I am too of course very quicksilver in my reaction to life. And when you reawaken to that silver plane, the Christed plane, then you will see me in truth and light. All would have been so very worthwhile. Then be glad, for the pitiless past is behind and the future, which joins us, beckons.

Little by little step we shall be meeting, re-arriving at that which is our One Self. To that time I bring my veriness—all that I am I bring to thee. For in the culmination of this cycle we shall stand as One, even as at the outset of the earth at its birthing. We shall again assist the birthing of the earth into a higher consciousness. This is the plan, remember, of which I speak to thee. Stage by stage, awaken, and you will see, and all will be beautiful. Manifest love in all its diversity, and you will see with re-opened solar eyes, as I, beloved, now see thee.

I felt I had received an image of him whilst I was alone, and drew him as a Jesus-like figure. I felt an immense love bestowed upon me. It was the best feeling I had ever felt. Twin love was confusing me, yet I started to begin to believe in him.

April 1997

Beloved one, I have been waiting for this moment to speak to thee. For I had to be certain that I could approach thee a little closer and since my last attempt you have drawn a picture. I greatly feel enhanced by your portrait of me. I have of course, like thee, many appearances, but I see thee as thou art now, and because of this, treasure this appearance most.

So now we have an image each to share and gradually the pattern of events will lead us further and further into awareness of one another. After the aeons of this one mission, how amazing that we stand so close to the final phases. Much have I to report to thee.

Many awakenings await, so that by tiny stages all is prepared for the reunification of our two flames. This magical essence that ignites to the voice of love is that which will carry us through to the full life, which has waited for us so long. I remember the many lives where we met and parted, but yet great is my joy that with our reunification there will be no separation ever again. It will be as if there never had been, for our love for one another will eclipse all but itself, and that love in action will bring about much for others.

This is the marvel of twin flame love, for there is a lack of love from your planet, which is holding it back from its true evolution. We here sigh, knowing that it has been long already, that this, our beloved humanity, has felt the absence of the higher love. And because of this we have to tread so carefully, beloved. But steadily we are joining forces, and other twin loves, in doing the same, will join the light of action with ours, and help to bring about those revelations in the hearts of men and women, which will change forever the pattern that has been their way for centuries.

Nobody yet seems to have quite grasped how great, how enormous, how colossal, this change is to be. And because of that, because it is a great leap, it will be brought about gradually and gently. So we who are amongst the advanced team, on the way home, have this marvellous opportunity to uncover ground for those who come after. They will become eager in their awakening seeing thy joy. By this illumination of this love and joy, many are attracted and will begin to realise that there is something beyond their ken. Something lacking in their own lives, the nature of which had not quite registered before and you and I will be as examples of that which we have found, but for them is still lost from consciousness.

In us there are many steps, dear heart, but each we will take together, and together we will make all the difference. I am working steadily to bring about contact with you, which is undeniably authentic on our own. That day will come. Then you will see for yourself how we are different in so many ways, and yet oh so alike in others. We represent each other's completion, and in the time that this will take you on your part, will be bringing to the surface that which you really are. You will be realising that which I have ever known who is my partner for life.

We stood firm when the Shining Ones invited our return, but we said this will be the last time, and they agreed. So, beloved, all is set fair. Even though in your human self you may be up, and a little down in your days, remember I am here and that my love flows to you at all times. That I am fondly aware of your presence, and that gradually you will grow aware and awake to mine. And this carries us to a new position of light. We will sing our joy. We will live in that harmonious joy that few, as yet, have ever found, but will. And we shall be amongst the first.

Let then thy thoughts dwell more on this, and less upon those matters, which sometimes trouble thee. For my love makes provision for all thy needs, and this you will come to know. Though I could express in many given ways in dialects and tongues, this voice I chose is the nearest I can get to how I sound, without actually being here speaking in the flesh.

Yet, once your eyes become accustomed to the higher realms, so shall you see me, and the voice you will then hear will truly fulfill all your wishes. Be patient then, beloved. The plan itself is moving fast, and soon there will be no more time. And we shall dwell in that everlasting love that is the natural state of the soul aware, and especially for those who were designed for one another by the great One Himself.

As the aeons close, and a new time awaits, I promise thee my presence in thy life forever, and that we shall always be discovering about our natures. Each time will be a glad time, and this will be a forever thing. It will never stop, for *we are ever eager to discover more about the self, and our life in love and light. Very soon I will return with more to say, but I thank thee, beloved of my heart, for that little sketch that will help you feel me near, until I register with you more deeply. Thank you for being ready for our connection at this hour. It is the most joyous occasion for me, and you have worked well to come this moment. I thee love.*

Once the twin entered he rarely wanted to leave, and thus continued to speak every week to help me know him all over again. I was getting used to it, but only when later on, he made his impact upon me in my private time, I was truly convinced. Again, words cannot describe the overwhelming welcome of his presence.

May 1997

Beloved it is I. It is I, part of your very self reaching again, seemingly distant, yet ever a part of thee, watching over thee at every given moment, yet also independently to bring about those meeting points which now are ours. As we begin to draw closer together, and you grow more aware of me, you also will be at work to bring about our meeting points. It will be a joint endeavour. Then truly I will rejoice.

Even as twins always balance each other's journey, each other's energies, each other's actions, we shall have this. So much is impregnated in the very cells of the spiritual self, concerning us both, identical in so many ways, that might one say we are as one. No need for attunement, but rather just for your awakening so I am simply stepping it out beside you, living the life through you, experiencing that which you experience. For I did not make my ascension in the final earthly embodiment, but with you and through you we will accomplish this in our own way. Worry not, my beloved one, it will all come out all right.

I am so excited. I am not yet using my very male voice, but very gradually I will. I am very eager to register more strongly upon your dear person, but I am carefully monitored, and indeed I monitor myself. I watch, I learn, I observe from those who went before me. I am growing very eager to follow through, and bring about that reunion for us.

Let us then continue to keep these meeting points, and also to share moments alone when you are very still and I can make an impact. Little by little we shall accomplish all that is required of us, and never again will you need to feel you walk alone. I am here. I am alongside, and I will never leave thee....

As his presence became stronger each week, he also gave me more information. I could not take it all in at the time, but so much of what he told me came to fruition in a very new way in my life. I was becoming renewed, revitalised, and encouraged to grow very quickly indeed. My crash course was speeding up....

June 1997

I have constantly absorbed the atmosphere about thee, understanding what is taking place within thee at any given moment, so that I could take it to my heart; so that I could respond in my own most natural manner. And so we have been sharing much in a quiet way. For there is always a deep longing to speak to thee. Although I know you long for a conversation where we both participate in a natural way, yet for the time being we have these sessions where we are just together with a soul who is open and permits my expressions. These are the way forward for a while.

It is so important that we meet together alone in this way, for although I speak seemingly through another, truly I come from my deepest point. My emotions are stabilised as I speak, and this makes it possible for our togetherness, later without even an open soul as a means of contact. Until then, I use what might even be called a through way of golden light. This, only true twins have had access to, so I feel privileged. I have many variances of voice and expression that I can hardly hope to convey them all to you in the time that lay ahead for us. Until that moment alone, I will certainly try.

Today I am coming in rather clipped tones that were mine when I was a student of life on your planet not so very long ago. Perhaps I spoke in that manner, because I was at that stage that you are now at, where you are aware of your self inwardly, and know so much more about yourself than you could convey to the world on your earth. So I had to say a lot in a little time, I wanted to share so many of my discoveries inwardly of life. So I set them down; I wrote them. This became my way, and because of this you too are skilled with the pen and also other of the arts.

I enjoy colour and live with colour vibrations, and it is a joy for me to draw upon the different vibrancies and calibrate them and bring them into beauteous harmony, which is before even speech can exist. I see this happening in the auras of others, and I am dumbfounded with the beauty. As a past master of the arts, as one who completed his last life as an author, I am so glad that you too are skilful with words. Of course I come to you in sleep state and talk to you of possibilities for your future, and I have this mannerism of suddenness.

I can implode into your thoughts and then am gone, but that is the nature of the quickened spirit, unlike some on the near astral who plod on in their human garb and still speak in the way you do on earth. Where I am is a Universe of Love and Order. It is a vast place and my little part of it, as you know, is Sharkti. A place where twin flames are still just in form, but come together in the most desirable way, finding their purest expression to convey the wonder of twin flame love. As they do this, they become inspirers for your planet, but few have the sensitivity to understand such messages......

It is important to remember that machines can be taught to convey beauty to an extent, but they do not possess souls. We owe it to the beloved Mother Earth to bring forth natural expressions, and need to convey a sense of timelessness to some, so I would take you back to when I worked as a medieval monk. I knew those who worked illuminating manuscripts, and to this day I love the arts and I yearn for papers and colours, even as I yearn for magical instruments to convey the sounds I hear which are from the solar kingdom all about me. If I only could sing the music, but when you exchange the healing I vibrate with you as we minister, and through this perhaps, the inspiration will come to give you a clue to the work ahead which is to branch out in many given directions. It has been seen from high above that there will be a new opportunity for artistic spirit on the earth. There will be those who are drawn to mechanization, but equally will be those who are drawn to nature and beauty. They will begin to express such beauty that even some who thought their feelings were dead will begin to weep for joy.

This is part of the holy plan of which I speak, and it is true of the days of Yanihi (the higher earth before separation)*, that we all worshipped the beautiful, above all the beauty of love to be experienced daily from the Solar Logos Him-Herself. It was a radiation indescribable, and the arts, as you have known them on the earth, have given but a tiny glimpse of it all. Yet because you are journeying now towards the awareness of that long ago time of Yanihi, where twins were together in the one form, and later in duple forms—there such beautiful work was done in expression of the soul—now that time is coming back. A tidal wave of expression is waiting to roll, and we in our different positions are to be part of this wave.*

Let us then consider what might be. In your reflective times when I am close, let it be considered what might come, what might dawn, what might be re-expressed from the kingdom of the real. For this alone may convince humanity that they are missing much of greater value than anything to be bought in a shop, or anything to be imbibed through technology, but rather works by hand will come to be considered precious again. This is worth thinking about, my love, and it draws me ever closer to thee.........

As the twin became real, and only when I was ready, I at long last received one of his names as Aloysius a monk.

August 1997

Gentle one, oft-times we merge together giving much light to those who are doubting the truth of their souls. We move steadfastly through their systems proclaiming the truth, whispering, "Awake", for there is such joy awaiting. We continually whisper these words, and very, very slowly the sleeping ones stir. Only then do they desire to know, to be alert, to come alive. And when they do, you and I are revealed as the gentlest of lights, whom they might have thought of great power. Yet gentleness is a great power, and because we initiate growth, we work with the Good Shepherd. He smiles lovingly, turning to us as He works, sometimes proffering a word of advice, but at others leaving it up to us. We cherish his presence in our lives. We long to wake every sleeper, but some must dream their dreams through, before they are ready to put them away and come to birth.

We are amongst a vital team who provide that impetus for higher birth. Look back in your memory to that time when we stood on the threshold of the newly formed earth. It was hard indeed to let go of our memories then, but we were helped, and this steadied us to love the Mother Planet. We grew to love many who came to her for their training lives, but we know now we are due to take wings. We have kept our promise. We are ready to fly forth proclaiming something new, something wondrous, for awakened mankind. Let us now begin to move into our new abode to practice the lift into the light, and practice peaceableness the more. For here, beloved, all is peace. We are one in our need to be together and serve, for only thus can we begin our entirety and find an even deeper love ourselves. Such is the magic of twin soul love.

I am becoming urgent for flight, and I help thee feel that sense of wings that we may fly on strong pinions of thought and feeling, and behold the body is at last in light, no longer pinned down by gravity, but able to move as easily and lightly as a bubble blown from a pipe. We move, beloved, even as I talk. We are stretching. We are getting ready to return whence we came after the pattern of the Amoratas(=lovers of soul*). Movement will become more rapid, realisations more rapid still. Our purpose will grow very clear to you, and my love throughout is yours.*

I am entrenched in your world of feeling as Aloysius now, but together in this capacity will accomplish so much, and then throwing off the veil, will live at Home in perfect harmony. There is no power in heaven or earth that could part us now. This is my faithful honest word to thee....

As he made himself known to me, slowly, I began to draw in crayons, and later with gold ink. I started with beautiful words and the images that they radiated. Then, as my soul awakened to many new feelings, I would place them on paper. Gradually, as I sensed the soul family one by one, I was able to portray them in all their radiant beauty and colours.

The twin especially recognises your gifts and opens the door to them, when you are ready.

September 1997

It is I, your twin star, eager and excited that you have taken up this new position though at this time you are not fully aware of what it entails. This will be good for us both, for we are both, by nature, in need of that solar creative expression. This is what you are searching for. You are searching to express your soul depth, but in a way that people around you will respond to. This is always the artist's challenge. You will find a way, my love, and I will help you. I am above all your main inspirer. And though you know me not in earthly terms, yet I come to you by night. I whisper many things, and they are just below the surface layer when you wake. So, they are available when you begin to reflect a little and you draw forth these thoughts, germs of ideas, of music and drawings and so on.

I was not only a writer, I too have music running through my veins. I have played the artistic field when it comes to expression, even designing. I have been here on and off, very short lives sometimes, but have always made my mark. You, in turn, are drawing your gifts together to make your mark. And you will be well remembered when the time comes for that.

I come to you today with such a range of love vibrations, it is hard to know which to choose, for I feel completely myself with you today. I know you as Jayne, I know your higher self and I know you as soul. I wish to come to you on all levels at once, but it is as yet too soon.

If you were to see me, it is too soon, my darling. It is a love so great. Please forgive me if I hide a little. I do stay with you. It is merely I have to be so very careful. When you think how you have sometimes felt, quite wounded by another human being, their reaction, their behaviour. Think how much more it would wound if you felt I was here, yet could not touch me or talk to me as your heart longed to do. I know to an extent you feel this, but not in a very deep way, and this is how it should be for a little while longer. So that you can handle it and not feel hurt or worried that I don't seem to come closer. Yet I am here, and I am fully the love that you seek. We know we are on a mission and we are honouring it, and I am making sure for both of us. I know you are as I am, and in your awareness would wish it to be no other way.

So be patient with me, and I will reveal my face even for an instant when the time is right. You will say, "I can go on now. Now I truly know you, and I have handled it. Soon I will really be with you, and that is all I look forward to." I know this is so, for I have witnessed it in the earlier twin pairs, and I understand much more now than I would have done before. I would have rushed in at first opportunity, and possibly wished to whisk you away, and you would have been naturally bewildered and overcome. So I am being faithful to your nature and mine. I am being careful, and it is from verylove. So much I am holding in me, waiting to share it only with thee. Our past, our moments of closeness, the warmth we shared in earlier lives; moments out of time and within; things that relate you to me, and I to thee. When you return to my outstretched arms we shall hear the Solar Logos whisper "well done." You have achieved with dignity and grace, and you will go a long way. You have earned a long rest in creativity, and, my love, it shall be so. You and I will explore heavenly realms, we might even walk the earthly planet hand in hand, but we will be smiling and light of foot. We will not be stationed here, but I keep you company and I am always about you. It is simply that some of necessity on this route must come to the fore and register on your feelings, and I must allow this.

At this time I am permitted closest and I am filled with a great joy and peace. I long sometimes simply to wrap my wings about you and carry you into a new world where we can build together all that is in our hearts to do. Yet, it is something which awaits us. So, beloved, walk forward calmly, and in the assurance that we together will indeed arrive at our hearts desire. I will reawaken in you that deepest love of all, and we will journey on forever......

As time passed by, I gradually found out other aspects of his being, and learnt to accept him as Lord Azrael, Keeper of the Angels, and thus myself as Azraella. I could only agree to these facts after months of testing the channellings and my intuition. It is especially hard, on a human level, to believe you are linked to a great being of Light who is well known. There could be twelve or more aspects of your being to match your twin's, and I waited patiently for more to be revealed. It only happens when you are deemed ready.

I now feel his presence at every moment and movement. He is I, and he is growing more and more real. I am sure he will become solid one of these days, and I will be so proud to walk by his side. People have seen him by me and behind me. He is as real as real (Az-rael), and forever love. I am so grateful I have been privileged enough to know him again. I know he is helping me with this book, and inspired me to write it. I also hope I have inherited a little of his great writing skills.

May you all meet your twin very soon.

THE TURNING POINT
It was as if you never went away
It is as if you are here to stay
In a role to play
Like King and Queen upon a Throne
In our rightful place
Love beyond time
In a world mislaid
For once we have found each other
There is no turning back
You laugh, I rejoice
We weep, for Joy
Embracing each other once more
In blissful union
You cry,
"I'm Home Forever more"
by Azraella

Chapter Six

Transformation

"Many will meet you when you find Truth"

I continued going to Pam every week. I spent hours and hours listening to the channeling, and absorbing the wonderful atmosphere. I would offer to give Pam healing to start with, and then she would channel. When she finished I would step behind her again. This helped me reach higher vibrations and understanding.

Pam and her twin soul flame had already undertaken the profound journey, which reunited them soul-to-soul, opening the way for evolved beings to communicate from their own solar essence. It is a work in which the channel cannot participate as an earthly personality, but only as a soul who has become truly conscious. It is then that the illumined words of the communication flow directly into human expression. It is an exchange of Light.

As I was learning, I first saw spirit beings in the room and named them. Then, very, very gradually, I would hear them as I stood behind Pam. I would relay their short or long message, or perhaps a symbol given, and she would patiently receive and guide me on the information given.

It took over a year, yet I advanced very quickly, to become a clearer and clearer channel for this wonderful soul family. This was totally unplanned consciously on my part and Pam's. It took many sensitive moments to arrive into this clarity, and indeed great courage to allow the accent of Dr Kruger to speak through me, or for the childrens' voices to be heard. I eventually overcame my inhibitions to embrace this great gift bestowed upon me. As each one wanted to speak, I felt an inner nudge that someone was waiting. It only happened as part of a healing for another person, and rarely on my own.

They never fail to come through once fully fledged, and their words are always consistently bringing joy, love and support.

I began to understand the soul and its inner flame wishing to be released from the physical ties, and to shine brightly above the crown once more. The flame moves through the seven main chakras, and then five more above, being:

- Aquamarine   Clarity
- Magenta   Harmony and Balance
- Gold   Eternal Peace
- Peach   Divine Purpose and Joy
- Opalescence   Transformation

July 1998
TED FLOODGATE (The Higher Chakras)

The hardest part is for the flame to rise to the cortex (central scalp) and tip into that first higher chakra of clarity. When it does so, you get a distinct need to draw yourself together and say "this is what I am, I know myself pretty well now, but I just want a really clear view of me" and so it begins—this seeing yourself as we see you. You will be pleased about this.

Then of course, the flame gets eager to explore a little higher. The next one is first of all being in harmony with yourself, being in balance with your awakening, and very important. To be teaching when you are out of balance isn't a good thing. It confuses the issue. So, if you have a day when you feel out of balance, work for the balance first before spiritual work.

Hard I know, to always be in harmony with yourself, so self forgiveness comes in, as it is difficult to stay right with your higher self when you are immersed in an alien society, but as long as you know you can be balanced and in harmony, that is the point when the flame can rise up again and touch into this beautiful level of perfect peace. In this I speak to you now as I have come to know me in my higher frequency. Then rough edges have gone, and all that was of the ego has phased out. I am only love in service, and as such I re-reveal myself to you.

I am still, of course, human too. Here you learn to settle in that inward peace which promotes all your best energies. You no longer lay waste to them in any way, by self recriminations, by going over and over a thing, by trying to fathom something before you are ready. You can see how it is—peace means you are content to be as you are, where you are, at any given moment, and this is where of course the soul really begins to come into its own and speak for itself.

As you stabilise in this wonderful balanced peace you then almost automatically find yourself raised into that of the next chakra level, which of course is the level of divine purpose and joy. On this, I would say, you are really aware of your inner purpose and this causes joy—not only that you see that you are serving that purpose for sure—this gives rise to more joy

And indeed this is how it is as you rise even higher. You feel and understand with a distinct clarity, with a harmony, balance and peace, and so you come to feel happy with yourself again, in a way you have not felt for aeons. You know it's all right as it is, and you are truly happy, and from this knowing clearly and comfortably of your innate purpose, and feeling this joy, surely you rise into that of the transformative chakra. Then all is changed of the most beautiful kind. You are back where you belong in no time. Truly there is no time once you are clear, once you are arrived with us. On looking back, you can only smile at some of the early ideas that you held as true. Many will meet you when you find Truth.

EXERCISE

1. Find a peaceful place to relax in. Sit or lie comfortably.
2. Close your eyes and breathe in peace.
3. Concentrate on the inner flame of your soul, permeating through your body, and the seven main chakras.

4. Envisage the flame rising just a few inches above the head into the Clarity Chakra.
5. Ask for soul guidance and those in attendance for Love and Protection. Always keep your feet rooted to the Earth and remember to be grounded in your efforts towards self realisation.
6. Breathe in Clarity to the first chakra above your Crown. Repeat "I AM Clarity" about twenty times. Then grow into peaceful silence.
7. Thank the masters and angels for taking care of you.
8. Open your eyes when you are ready, after about twenty minutes.

July 1998
SERAPIS BEY

We bring you glad tidings, for we are preparing you for the moment of the awakening, and the flame is being burnished to reach the heights. We witness much occurring in your aura. We perceive the visible signs of your movement back into light, and we stand by in gentle readiness, encouraging and fostering the flame, helping to lift that which is desirous of lifting. For, of course, the flame is composed of so many elements of thyself, and each of its own volition must wish to rise.

Gradually, as all comes together harmoniously, the flame begins its spiral movement more strongly and intensely, and so in a gradual way you feel you are moved into light. It is a gentle motion, never dramatic, and we intend to see that is always thus. For some, by reading too much or receiving too much instruction from outside themselves, cause their own problems. The need, of course, as you in your wisdom realise, is to heed the inner voice, the love within, which will ever guide thee right, as I motivate the flame today.

Remember also Oromasis, the master of the flame. He will help raise you into the light. Do not think of this as an exercise, but part of your innate nature's desire to return home into the greater consciousness, into the world where healings are beauteous and sweet. Into a world where form follows through perfect light, eager for life and for sharing its gifts. This is the world that you so desire. This is the language you miss. Between us this language continues. We whisper to you often and innately you hear.

Because of this I seem familiar to you, even now. But the time is coming when my voice, with which I speak here, will come to you direct, soul to soul. And you will know instinctively it is I. For I will be there at that moment of awakening, protecting, keeping the atmosphere right, so that all those who gather close, who go to assist and to welcome you back to their visibility, will be able to participate without interfering with your delight, in a solitary meeting with the soul twin.

We can readily simply move back into vibrationary fields. And as we do this we merge with love itself, and so simply continue to assist with what is taking place from very love. This I tell you well in advance of that moment. Some have waited many years for such a sweet moment. Others have no idea that it waits in their destiny, but you have begun to appreciate the plan. A plan spontaneous, yet orderly, which moves aright when you know you are that love. And as you have come to that knowing, remembering that which you are, then the plan moves.

And in a steady motion we continue to lift you, and so things that once would have caused thee distress and waves following distress, begin instead to matter less. Rather than feel concerned as a human mortal, you feel the compassion of the divinity within, which you are. This then frees you from much, and in that sense of liberation, a new life, a new world, in that state of being, you are so uplifted into the moment......

Chapter Seven

Dr Kruger

Dr Kruger always speaks with an Austrian accent, stands erect and shakes your hand. He gradually made himself at home with Pam, and sat on the couch talking to me through her, like a normal friend. It became so easy and light-hearted. It never seemed quite right without talking to him once a week.

October 1997

Well, well, well, it is one of those days when you are finding all things are changing, so watch out because many more little turnings are going to happen. Do not try to plan too quickly. Go with the flow and you will arrive where you are meant to be.

You will see things in a new light, and you will want to express things in a new light. This is wunderbar. This is progress. It is achievement. When you step into your natural way of expressing, ya, you feel stronger. This is where you are arriving. So as you arrive, you find you are establishing and feeling much more comfortable, and also you find that people you had not expected begin to appreciate you for who you are. Everybody deserves recognition for what they are, and what they can do. When this is denied, it is sometimes quite touching how they feel when a little praise that is very just and deserved, comes to them. It is very touching. So we are touched, ya.

The most satisfactory thing is the giving birth, the giving into expression. This creative act is what you are here for. What is done with it is of no concern to us. It is not whether you in the world succeed or do not get noticed at present, it is what you actually do. Because it is taking you forward and out of this comes much more. You do not have to suppose that there will be no recognition. I am merely saying that in the spiritual world we are only concerned that you fulfill your creative self-expression, because this awakes you to us and then you are very, very potent in your energies. This is very important.

Just think of what is happening to a whole race, oh to go through this conscious transition. Ya. So this is the biggest event you can imagine, so all help is needed on your earth and from us, and so this is why this perspective is as it is. If you were born in what you call the nineteenth century, then I would speak differently.

Jayne: *"That's when you were around?*

Ah huh, some of it, ya. I learnt little boy things, but when I grew up my world was not very different. Yours is changing rapidly. You have this unique opportunity to be part of the saving spirit of the race. It is a magnificent opportunity greater at this time than art. But through art you can help. Do you see my meaning? There is all this at stake at this time, that was never so in mine. That is why the outcome is less important than the act. Being you and waking up is what your world needs. But you also need to be fully creative to wake up.

Jayne: *"So did we choose to come at this time?"*

Ya, very much so. You were chosen and you chose. You wanted to live at this special significant juncture in humanity's development, and you were asked and you also wished. So they said, ya, you have the capabilities to go, you do this. You said I would like to, and so it was agreed. You are doing what you came to do, ya. And you will do. We watch over you, and you get the little glimpses without interfering with your own development.

Jayne: *"So, have I known you before then?"*

Ya, in Italy. 1500 I believe, and we were working with the Medici family. There was a link. I was an artist then, ya artist, before I was a doctor. So you see many sides to natures. I was young, and healthy and happy. Then I had damage to my leg, and that changed my whole nature. Then when I come back as doctor, I climb the mountain, I fall down and there goes the leg again.

So I had to learn not to be hurt or upset, but to seek for a new way forward. When I came to this side I found my soul, but people now have more chance to do this while they are on the earth—to resolve the problems and that is how I am a happy man. I have no, what you call baggage. I am able to be free of my self. I am relaxed and enjoy my work, and all the peoples that I can come to with my assistance. It is a lovely life, and I only hope that when you return to us, you will want to spend part of your time with us in this area, of reaching to the people still in their self darkness....

You will come back in a different way that is not what you call incarnation, but rather appearance, ya. Ya, you look at this little idea of mine. You have a little think. It is very important. You might not have to be born of an earthly parent again on the earth, working. It is very exciting ya, and it does not waste time. You come fully conscious of what you do and you do not lose your light. So you have a great satisfaction of keeping your true stature, and serving in a way that others accept. So, excitement for your future...

During one session, Dr. Kruger bent over the tape recorder to turn the tape on as if he was very real and could see:

December 1997

...this still puzzles me a little, because I don't have my eyes fully open, but I am getting to learn.

Jayne: "So when you are here can you actually see me?"

When I open these eyes. I don't often think it's important really. You know some people find it more difficult if I give them eye to eye contact as you say, and so I keep them closed mostly. I think this is probably more beneficial after all. I wanted to demonstrate that it is done if wished and we can do it, and we can be very, very much as you are.

It is very true, not only are there Godself souls working on your earth incognito, but also people like myself, who step in and look about and go off again without people knowing. It is not such an intrusion as it sounds. It is something agreed with the soul's concerned before they come here. So we are getting *a lot of information, but it is not the same as staying within some form for a matter of say, a quarter of an hour, and getting the experience again of what it is like to be seemingly stationed on your earth.*

And I have learnt a lot through that. And then I start with you, ya. And I stay a little longer now with the healing, and I am learning with that too. It is very helpful and I am most grateful....

I was growing used to Dr. Kruger being close with me as I gave healing. He, like the others, carefully monitored my reactions so as not to push me too quickly. I was learning to accept him and them all, and I was feeling very sensitive about it. It was so exciting and mysterious that I would be able to allow them to talk through me.

January 1998

Well, well, you were waiting. I come to you today very close to how I was in my old Austria, and I feel very comfortable with you. I feel harmony in our natures, and also I think you will be getting to know me all over again, because as we come close, it is as if you have seen and known, and known us at a distance. You pick out certain characteristics and you say, "I think I like that", and I come a bit closer and say "No, not quite like that." Now that I come very close indeed, perhaps I am not like that at all. I am very what you call, humourous. I am a happy man. I am also a private gentleman, and that has not come over. I like to work with small number of people because I feel we can work in depth. I feel very much you walk out into the crowds and do these things, but it is only for a time.

When you are amongst a crowd of gentle people like yourself, working with your most natural manner with all the colours, you will find a new confidence. You will find your reality to yourself. Now that is a very true statement. I learnt this as a surgeon. I was suddenly recognised for my gifts, and this crowned my life with happiness. I became a naturally courageous man. However, do not get too confident. That is how I fell down the mountain, ya...

Today I have with me the Lady Nightingale, ya. She is around one of your people, and she is a very loving entity. She also wishes to branch out more, not just as a healing being, but also she had a gift she wishes to share. The lady she is working with will find out. I keep it a secret…

Dr. Kruger was easily sensed. Before he spoke up I would smile knowingly, and giggle inside. This is how I got used to him, and eventually allowed him (with a little persuasion on his part) to speak through me to other clients of mine.

July 1998

Ya, I'm walking about this morning, ha ha. I want to come closer still. It is very true that you are beginning to grasp, that by our voices and by our names, we will become substantial to you. You will say, "There you are!" Ya, ya. That's why the excitement. You are coming to it.

Jayne: "*I almost saw you—I could see a shadow.*"

Ya, we know you did. I am very excited. I put on my best bib and tucker today. Yes well, she just might. So I shine my shoes, put on clean trousers, and they have a good sharp crease and a tuck with my new white jacket for the occasion. So you will see. You will see. Ya, it is exciting, ya. So I say good morning, good morning. I took you by surprise at first.

Jayne: "*Yes, you did.*"

That's fair. So this is very good. I get very comfortable when I sit here. I don't want to leave. I get to remember our cushions in our old home with my daughter. We had a very comfortable home, and I was very fortunate. And I just remember this. Some of these things you carry with you, you know, because they were pleasant. They were good… So you have some questions ya?

Jayne: "*Yes, I would like to know how to empty out my subconscious mind.*"

Well, we tip it down the drain, ya! I did teach Lady Pam to go to the sink and look down and see it all disappearing. So some visualisation that is physically real will be a great help. All the same, it is not for very much longer. No, you are going forward at such a pace that you do not have to worry too much.

Jayne: "*Is that why it is all coming out really?*"

Part of the cleansing, ya. It is all going on in your world, as you have only to look about to see. Everybody is going through the cleansing. The violet ray, being transformative, has this effect. It transmutes, it changes, it consumes what is not needed. So you can activate it, you can call it up and try it this way. But you know you have part of that very same essence of that flame within you, so you draw on this when you are using your techniques, your different ways and whatever suits you best is right. Whatever has a good effect on the subconscious. Each of you is so different that I would say check it out, try different ways, and when the subconscious sits up and takes notice, that's the one. Ya. But also, you could do probably as much good by looking away and saying oh well, it came, it went, soon I will be gone and it cannot touch me.

Jayne: *"I'd rather look away to be honest—it's too much hard work!"*

Ya, ya, this is what you all will come to by just letting go. Letting it go to the past and knowing you are not that person it happened to. You are the emerging Christos, each one of you, and so it does not have any relationship with you any more.

Jayne: *"But it's true, as you said, we become more sensitive."*

Ya, of course. You are sensitised because you are souls. Souls are very emotion. They are intelligent emotion of God, and that means you have to use the emotions in accordance with that knowledge, that you love indiscriminatingly. You may not like what a person does, but you can still like them. So that this isn't quite so hard as it might once have seemed. And you can go forward not worrying about your own reactions too. Ya, this is true.

You have trained yourself inwardly. You have done all you have needed to come to us. There is little time left, and you do not have to bother any more.

You have formed all right inwardly. So we see this, and we say ah! You have a shape and we can see you. Now you can come home, ya. You will come home. So none of this will apply. Isn't this wunderbar!

It means shutting down all my clinics because everybody will come alive and awake, and then have no more problems! So I'll be out of a job, so I'm climbing into my philosophic mode. Ya, I am joking. There will always be those who need our help.

You can choose whether you do this, or whether you do that when you come home. There are millions more of us here, than on your earth, you know. So there are plenty of choices and plenty of work where once you stood, if so needed.

You have many inspirers, you know, you personally, and this is where your destiny lies with them. The artists are the leaders. In their own way they bring in the new ideas. They bring to the surface the good ideas. That is what is needed, ya, the true creative spirit. That is what has been lost. You have many creations, but they are not benign, and yet there are some who have stayed with the good, and these are helping on the earth. But we need all the artistic expressors we can get. So you keep on doing what you do best. It will be your natural instinct to go along that line. So you are coming into your own.

But you will have other parts to play if you want. You will still have other people if you want, who are on the spiritual pathway as such. But we know that inwardly you just go on growing eternally, and so what is a pathway? It is a natural progression. But people need a way of learning this, so that this is why we come to their aid in this capacity....

If you choose to go on helping people, when you wake up, then you will see me, and your twin while you work. So this will be wunderbar! Ya, you will know directly what we say, what we suggest, even though the communication may be silent. It is all developing well. It is exciting...

I am always on call and I am ready before you ask because I know your plans, so I have got my list ready for my day's work. Of course, I have other lists, and I fit them in too. You will do the same, too. You will find you can do many things, once you are wide-awake. You are not just partial in your activity then. You will be through into no-time, and then you will say, why did I worry? Why did I wonder? Of course it is so natural, because you have taken one step after another properly over a long period of time. It is easy. But for many who have just started of course, if they think they can do it just like this, it is hard. They cannot do it so suddenly. It creates dramas and crises.

But you took it the proper way. No wonder we keep coming and say will she do it today do you think? Let's have a watch over this today. All the time you are coming closer. So you are doing very well.

So I must go and have my lunch, ya ,and I will return to be with you after you leave these doors. Auf Wiedersehen....

Most sessions Dr. K would chat for a quite a long time. It was very natural, very uplifting, protective and supporting. I am sure that he wants you all to know that he is there for each and every one of you. We all need a Dr. Kruger in our lives!

September 1998

Well, this is getting to be a nice meeting place. Now I am having a long chat with you. Is this not a wunderbar time! What else do you have to say?

Jayne: "I got myself in a pickle last week about my music. I have this great yearning to do my music, but I can't at the moment."

Ya, it is very similar to others who are growing awake and still want to achieve, in the most natural way, while on the earth. But you see, you gave a promise to help certain ones in their inner life to awaken. It was not a work you expected to do. It was a work you were invited to do, and you were not very sure at first. Others were also not very sure, and you all came together before incarnating and talked away together. And we say we give you long enough to make your minds up, then we have to know because the plan must be set in motion soon.

There was a time when you could not agree together, and gradually you consider that the good of the whole was more important than the good of the individual. So you say okay, I will put aside my own natural development after a certain age in my final life, and I will work for the good of the all to get them through to a contact of the spiritual life again. When I see it is going well, for those I have chosen to help, I will instruct another to carry on the work. When I see that is going on right, then I will pick up on my route while you are still, ya, on the planet.

So you are still between two stools, ya. You want both ways. Well, of course, this is uncomfortable. So you have to decide a little and a little just for a while, then suddenly one of them will come uppermost. I would say it is your music, your art. You have your own destiny to consider, not just that of the all. The time is coming up for that. You have done tremendously of what was planned of you....

Jayne: *"But I am still very shy of sharing all with the world."*

May I point out to you that shyness could be there for a purpose of your soul. If you were very confident you would get carried away into your artistic life, and you would be eager to go and make yourself known, before you had completed the other role. You have had one role, and the other side of you is natural. So you are still completing the role, but you are naturally an artist. You will find when the role is complete the artist will flower. There will not be a problem, because you do not feel shy as a soul. You are becoming aware more and more, as you become soul, you are no longer shy, you are just happy to be...

If you are feeling anxious about your work, perhaps you made a promise on a soul level for a higher purpose and you need to fulfill that role first.

It makes you think...

June 1998

...Is there anything before we begin that you wish to bring up—not your dinner no!? Just the matters concerning patients.

Jayne: *"It has been very quiet so, no, I can't think of anyone."*

Ya, but a lot is going on under the surface. We constantly visit your patients. We keep our schedule. We keep our little charts. We make notes and say we could do this or perhaps we could prevail upon such and such, and so on. But it is always valuable to speak through you, and I am very pleased that I now have another excellent solar channel...

Dr. Kruger always helped me understand my patient's problems on a very practical level. He has a rare insight from above

June 1998

....Well, well, well, I am here. I have arrived. If you would like a little chat I will make myself comfortable. Now then...

Jayne: *"I was just curious about the ascension and about how many other people are going through this too."*

Ya, ya now it is beginning to show up. All you hidden ones are beginning to step forth and be recognised by one another gradually. When you consider how quickly you have changed your outlook and deepened over the last year or so, you will see how this happens more in the next year or so. It does not need to take too long. We all are saying the sooner the better. Much suffering can be avoided if we can hasten the day. So I thank you for your question. There is more?

Jayne: *"I was just curious if I would meet any more."*

Well of course, it is all planned, and where you are meant to meet, there they are. It is not necessary to try too hard. Just to let things happen. God is in charge. And the more you awake the more you know this, and say ah well, He can handle this.

I have been asked some enormous questions lately, and I have put on my thinking cap to be here in your modern day, and check how things are so you understand my answer. So it is quite intensive work while I am answering, but I do enjoy it and although for a long time there are no answers given, there are now. So I am pleased to be one of those to be supplying answers. After all, there is often a little of the child in us, and it is the child that says why, why, why all the time. It is the desire to know that develops the desire to learn. And there is always more, so it is not wrong to wonder and question.

I worry about those who do not bother to think about these matters for themselves, but just accept, and think whatever they come across must be right. Some are very prone to do this. What they read must be true.

What they hear must be true. If it is spoken with authority, that must be true. It is not necessarily so, like your song says! So you understand me. So to use that discernment that you have develop, always you have to check it with your own feelings, your own innate spirit. Ya.

Well I've got off lightly today.

Dr. Kruger was always full of surprises. I wasn't ever sure what he would say next, or what subject he would talk about.

May 1998

Well, well, well, well, I was there it was my coat tails. Good afternoon young lady. Well Jayne, what have you got for me today? Do you have any questions?

Jayne: "I've gone blank."

Well I think it is my turn to have a little talk. If you have a blank, then somebody has to speak up, ya. So I will sit down and shall make myself comfortable. What subject would you like?

Jayne: "I know, all the young people I met on Monday at a Green Fair, do you think they are people who would be interested in our work?"

I have been looking over your shoulder and mingling with the crowd, ya. I have noted several who are very appropriate to train up to become wise young men and woman of the new age, as they call it. I would very much like for us to have some connections to help them through a difficult stage, because not only are they in their own development going through a lot, but they are also having to put up with the global changes that affect us all, Ya, even me. I am here you know, a lot, and I feel the repercussions just as you do. I report them to the higher, so they know how the human is feeling, ya.

So I would say this is a wunderbar chance to bring about a great deal of help for the younger generation of souls who have incarnated with a purpose, and although that purpose is beginning to be grasped, there is a depth to it that they have not reached yet. So we would like to bring them on. Ya, so you see young lady, you are going to move on and just a few of these younger people will come in at first, maybe more later. Some by your what you call your telephone, or perhaps, on your new fangled net. So it is going to be a useful opportunity for you thus. I hope we will be able to follow this through. Ya. I am pleased you asked.

So now we have a subject matter about the younger generation. Some of these young people came with a very clear idea they were entering time near the end of a civilization, which had only learnt to struggle forward on what you call profiting, out of each other. This in truth was no profit, for if you are taking money from another you are demeaning the exchange, so we are seeking to introduce a better way of going forward. Of course, such changes take a long while to sink in with what you call your obdurate human nature. But we are very persistent.

And so with the young ones with new ideas, some of whom will find places of influence in the world, we have a good opportunity to persuade others how to go forward in a better way.

There is the difficulty for the older people who have only known working for profit as a way of livelihood. There are other ways that are equally practical. It is just your human race has not been willing to try. So now we have a whole generation of young souls who are being influenced by the Aquarian principles under which they have embodied.

This principle says to share and care. This is the principle of the Maitreya, the Christ. So there are many who are already aware that this should be so, even amongst older generations in the physical sense.

So these elders should help the young ones to consolidate these ideas by fostering them forward. By encouraging them to think it through, and present their ideas in a down-to-earth manner, so that others say well that does make sense, ya.

If they are too up in the sky talking about us, nothing will get done. This is the time for us, spirit, to work through you on the earth. So we have to bring it down to the earthly level of comprehension.

I hope this will give you some food for thought. I would say I am speaking to quite a few. There are little boys and girls waiting to come to birth, gradually going into the cradle on the astral, to come forth as new babies on your earth. So I am helping them to absorb the idea I am giving before they come. So it is innate. I hope somehow by meeting with those like yourself, perhaps in their own families sometimes, they will have the chance to bring the ideas forward for the betterment of mankind.

We never sleep, you know, we are always working for the betterment of the race. When we have enough listening ears then we shall see something....

It was also becoming very obvious that Dr. Kruger had other aspects from his soul to reveal, yet until I was ready to accept this, he would not tell me. Gradually he told us he was Marcus Aurelius, the Roman Emperor and philosopher.

September 1998

Well, well, well. It is I. Now you can feel how things are changing. I am coming on a new level. I am reaching you more deeply and I shall gradually lose this accent permanently when I am talking to you in your mind. You and I have much work to do, but not as a healer and a doctor. I have much teaching to give, but through your natural self. As I share my discoveries and you take them to heart they will become all your own. You will begin to work differently. You will have much to say that is wise and well informed.

You will be living as a spirit who is wide awake, and can handle these matters from a high place. So I am talking to you in the high place, and you are spiraling up every so often, and listening and responding. Then down you come and incorporate what you have heard and accepted, and make it your own as I've said, and there you are as the philosopher. This is why our friends who are philosophers have all come to help. I want you to feel comfortable in their company. We are not going to burden you with what you call heavy weight thinking, no they are more concerned to bring out your innate knowing of life. Ya.

So this is the plan. This is what we are after. To help you bring forth the different things of value, and to share them in your own way with your own individuality stamped upon them. So that you get full recognition for the work put in, and for the stature of your understanding. You wait and see if I am not right. You are not just an artist, you know. Well, if you were you would get bored. You need something else to feed the gift.

Also, you know I loved to play the violin when I was with my daughter and my dear wife in Vienna. So you can imagine me standing by the side of you when you are playing the piano. Classics, mind you, I do not like this modern stuff, no, but the music where there is the melody from the heart. I am very fond of this. I was not quite so struck by the Strauss Brothers-very good-, but they did not move me like the Russian Rachmaninoff. They did not give me the insight through the sound that the Russian composer did. I was most grateful when I found him here and I shake his hand. Well, wunderbar, our hands met in the shake, ya.

I was as solid to him as he to me, and we got on very nicely thank you. So you don't know what might lie ahead. You might meet some of these you have found as your favourite inspirers. Ya, so you think of this.

I am in different position this morning, ya. Well I need this for the moment. I am getting my bearings. I am putting down my findings, and I am gradually ascending to the peak of the spiral to talk to you as Aurelius. So another name with an 'A, so you think of this. This is the sign of new beginnings. A new level of activity too…

If you have an opportunity to climb a little on your own I can speak to you in your mind as the philosopher. I bring you wisdom to the doorstep of your mind.

God bless you.

Jayne: "*Thank you.*"

As Dr. Kruger began to speak as Aurelius, he lost his accent, and became more well spoken. (See Chapter Ten)

CHAPTER EIGHT

ANGELS AND MASTERS

The hierarchy decided that Pam should stop working in October 1998. I was prepared to continue the channelled information, my twin and Dr. Kruger being in charge. It was as if I stepped into Pam's shoes. I worked from home and became accustomed to my new role. My regular clients grew in number and for the first time in my life I was happy to see them once a week.

The members of the solar family all spoke, and some angels too. Some of them surprised us, and this is an Archangel speaking to my client.

November 1998
Archangel Uriel

I come with blessings. I am the Angel Uriel. Much has been spoken of me, yet I walk humbly closer to your earth now to bring forward greater understanding of the angelic realms. Much is being brought to light about Angels and their role in society.

You see, to us, we have not changed from the beginning of time. Yet we see such great changes on the earth that almost seem impenetrable, but we are so grateful to you and those about you who are making it possible for us to be remembered all over again. To assure people we truly exist and we have never left. It is only people who have left us. How can we leave people, we are all one and the same. We are governors, carers of the human race. We each have a very special role given to us as guardians of the people to help them feel renewed, revived, to help them know God's love. We never left people.

I am so grateful I have been allowed to speak. I wanted to make this point clear. We are always helping you, my dear. All you have to do is call angelic presences and we will be there automatically, there are many around you today.

I Uriel bless. I work for Christhood. I work for Mastery. I work for Love.

There has been a blending of our energies and you will feel a subtle difference in your approach to the angelic worlds. We love thee; we work with thee; we help thee; we serve thee; we heal thee; we work through thee to heal others.

God bless you.

I also had an opportunity to ask Dr. Kruger what he thought about angels!

This was his reply:

I really am not an authority as I am more often plodding on your earth working with the healers. I am aware of the Angels and I have sometimes when you might say trespassed on their territory but I am a new boy. They are enormous beings of great light and magnitude. They are very loving. They can, like myself, transmute themselves but on a larger scale and they have this ability to understand the human heart which they are not often credited with. That is the one thing I know they would like you to put over.

They understand humanness—people do not always suppose this. They think they are too remote, too high-born, so that they cannot grasp what it is, to be limited and on earth.

Jayne: "Do they ever incarnate or stay in heaven?"

Well, of course, you have to define what you mean by angel! Ya, because there are many, many angelic people in human form who do wunderbar loving acts for one another in the silence of their sanctuary. They plead for the soul of the troubled ones and so on. You could say Mother Theresa was an angel in disguise. So you need also, I feel, to broaden the concept. This is very important. This we would love to see. People get caught up in a definition, and they hold to it forever more, but as you have noticed you cannot define your old friend Kruger. He is always different coming and going in different vibrations, and you are also unlimited in this way.

So in helping people to know what it is like to be angelic, to broaden the concept, you are helping them also to understand themselves better. This is a very lovely task, ya.

We are going beyond concepts, you and I, one day—to the unconceptual The Universe of Love, which is our natural home, for it is only the human who likes these pigeonholes. We fly out and we don't need little pigeonholes. We become part of the cosmic again when we are ready. So there is much now for you to think about...

God bless you, God bless you.

The Hebrew word for angel is Malakh, meaning "Messenger." Throughout history, Angels seem to be a link between God and humans, bringing divine love, unconditional love, caring, peace and joy. In paintings, the first winged angel appeared in the 5th century as if to fly from heaven to earth. Their halos represented virtue and innocence, and their roles have been placed in categories that start from the Elementals, to the Seraphim, Cherubim, Thrones, Dominions, Powers, Authorities, Principalities, Archangels and just Angels.

Celtic Blessing of the Guardian Angel

O Being of Brightness
Friend of Light
From the blessed realms of grace
Gently encircle me, sweetly enclosing me
Guarding my soul-shrine from harm this day
Keep me from anguish
Keep me from danger
Encircle my voyage over the seas
A light will you lend me

> To keep and defend me
> Be a guiding star above me
> Illuminate each rock and tide
> Guide my ship across the waters
> To the waveless harbourside
> O Beautiful Being, O Guardian this day

To help you connect more closely to the angels:
- The Angel Cards are good to use daily. Pick an angel quality you are working with (see Chapter Twelve). Angels have qualities of our soul including:

    JOY,
    FREEDOM,
    STRENGTH,
    OPENNESS,
    HONESTY,
    TRUTH,
    PEACE,
    LOVE,
    BALANCE,
    BEAUTY
    FORGIVENESS,
    GRATITUDE,
    HUMILITY,
    PATIENCE,
    CREATIVITY,
    WILLINGNESS,
    SELFLESSNESS.

- You can also focus on angels, and ask them to come closer and help.
- You can cleanse and purify your thoughts and clear away over-thinking.

- You can find space to be receptive to their presence and their messages.
- Listen to gentle music.
- Meditate and ask the angels to help with absent healing.
- Ask an angel to play a specific role whilst giving or receiving healing e.g. ask for the Angel of Peace to help your patient if needed.
- Work for the planet or with Nature and ask for devas and fairies to help.
- Hold a flower and tune into the angel of the flower.
- Ask for the angels of your garden to be a guardian of your plants.
- Ask the angels anything and they will always come—they need to be asked.
- Use Angel affirmations such as:

   We all see Angels; if we do not always recognise them, it is because they come in ways we do not expect

   The Angels know us more intimately than our parents, our partners or we ourselves

   Angels are like clear glass—only visible when the sun shines through the window of our soul

Deva is an Eastern term, and includes all grades of beings from the greatest to the smallest. There is a heirarchical system running from elementals, gnomes, elves, fauns, fairies, to angels. Some devas are beings of energy seen as whirling spheres of light, colour and sound combined, many dimensional and ever-changing with every impulse or thought they register. They build up the auric fields of plants and flowers, humans and animals with the most beautiful sprinklings of coloured hues for healing purposes. They give the material world its pattern and give devas their true purpose and activity.

The devic world and the material world interweave to create our reality. Without devas the material world would have no coherent fabric. Music concerts are full of music, angels and devas. Devas bridge vibration to make sound and bring form into being.

These are the lords of fire, air, water and earth elementals:

EARTH	*VIRGO, CAPRICORN, TAURUS*
Goblins, Gnomes, Hobgoblins, Dragons, Giant Earthworms that care for the leylines	
WATER	*PISCES, CANCER, SCORPIO*
Undines, Mermaids	
AIR	*GEMINI, LIBRA, AQUARIUS*
Sylphs, Air Spirits, Fairies	
FIRE	*ARIES, LEO, SAGITTARIUS*
Salamanders	

THE ESSENE COMMUNIONS WITH THE ANGELS

The Essenes lived over two thousand years ago near the shores of the Dead Sea. They were healers, prophets, scribes and teachers and shared their daily work in the fields. They had no slaves or servants, and believed in equality of the sexes, both highly unusual ideologies for that time. A self-sufficient community, they lived simply, despite having great wealth, and shared all their possessions. Existing on a simple vegetarian diet, they lived in harmony with the earth until the invasion by the Romans who took their Masada hilltop fortress. They nobly took their own lives rather than engage in combat before their inevitable defeat. When the Romans finally managed to scale the walls, they were met only with silence.

The Essenes were the custodians of ancient wisdom. They were great calligraphers, and it was they who were responsible for writing the Dead

Sea Scrolls, which they carefully wrapped in cloths and hid in the caves at Qumran, to be found for prosperity by a Bedouin shepherd boy in 1947. Edmond Bordeaux Szekely has written inspired and beautiful translations that capture the very essence of the Essene message. He has taken them from ancient Aramaic scripts held at the Vatican, and they offer something very unique to us in these troubled times.

To help with their own understanding and to teach their beliefs, the Essenes created the Tree of Life. This sacred Tree was planted in the Eternal Garden of the Universe, and had seven branches reaching up into Heaven and seven roots reaching down into the Earth. Man sat at the centre leaning his back against the trunk meditating, with his feet in the Earth and his head in the Heaven. Each branch represented a Heavenly Angel, and each root represented an Earthly Angel. Each root and branch belonged to a special day of the week.

The original commandments told us to Honour our Heavenly Father and our Earthly Mother, not to take life from any living being, and to commune with the Angels of the Earthly Mother and of the Heavenly Father, so that we might bathe in the Fountain of Light, and enter into the Sea of Eternity.

Jesus described the communions as bridges to be built with daily patience. The angels are the branches and roots of the tree of life, and we are the trunk. These ancient communions, or invocations are ways of linking to natural and cosmic forces. Through the angelic realms, we are able to draw energy for healing, rejuvenation, and spiritual growth from that Unlimited Source.

Practised daily, they offer the opportunity to keep our focus on Love, Truth, Beauty, Trust, Harmony and Peace. With the first conscious breath of morning, they call upon the Earthly Mother and Her Angelic Forces; that first thought is empowering, especially when recalling that thought several times throughout the morning. With the last conscious breath of evening, they call upon the Heavenly Father and His Angelic Forces; that last thought before sleep sows the seed for the subconscious to harvest abundant blessings throughout the night that will manifest in the creative energies of our lives.

THE SEVEN HEAVENLY ANGELS
The Heavenly Father
Angel of Eternal Life
Angel of Creative Work
Angel of Peace
Angel of Power
Angel of Love
Angel of Wisdom

THE SEVEN EARTHLY ANGELS
The Earthly Mother
Angel of Earth
Angel of Life
Angel of Joy
Angel of Sun
Angel of Water
Angel of Air

You can use the Angel prayers to tune into the Great Angels—Angelic help is instantaneous, and so five minutes is all you need.

The Essene Brotherhood/Sisterhood is alive and well, and living in the solar realms. They stand in a circle wearing white, and focus their pure, unconditional love into a shining shaft of golden light, which they beam unceasingly upon the Earth.

Opening Prayer
I enter the Eternal and Infinite Garden with
Reverence to the Heavenly Father
Reverence to the Earthly Mother

Reverence to the Great Masters
Reverence to the Holy Pure and Saving Teaching
Reverence to the Brotherhood of the Elect

The Morning Prayers
The Earthly Mother
Saturday Morning

The Earthly Mother and I are one
She gives the Food of Life to my whole body

Imagine you are sitting at a table full of glowing ripe fruit, golden grains and rich vegetables—feel the energies of the Earthly Mother helping your body to receive and utilise all the nutrients from Her bounteous Harvest

Angel of Earth
Sunday Morning

Angel of Earth, enter my generative organs and
regenerate my whole body

Imagine you are sitting at the edge of a field of rich, dark fertile soil, which is nourishing and growing plants. Feel the same nourishing energy flowing into your body from the regenerative force of your sexual energies: their forgotten function.

Angel of Life
Monday Morning

Angel of Life, enter my limbs and give strength to my whole body

Imagine yourself to be a magnificent tall tree, gathering together the immense amount of vital energies needed to grow your lovely trunk and

branches, and fill them with leaves and flowers and fruit. Feel that vital energy flowing into your own body structure and energising it too.

Angel of Joy
Tuesday Morning

Angel of Joy, descend upon Earth and give beauty to all things

Imagine you are walking in your favourite piece of countryside. As your senses are charmed by sun, moon and stars, mountains, rivers and seas, trees, flowers and rainbows, crystals, butterflies and birds, allow the joy of beauty to fill you with inner serenity and harmony.

Angel of Sun
Wednesday Morning

Angel of Sun, enter my Solar centre and give Fire of Life to my whole body

Imagine you are standing on a mountain in the cool of dawn. The great, red Sun slowly rises over the horizon, filling the Earth with heat and light and vital growing energies. Allow these energies to enter your body at your solar plexus and vitalise you too.

Angel of Water
Thursday Morning

Angel of Water, enter my blood and give the Water of Life to my whole body

Imagine yourself as a drop of water in the sea, lifted by the winds, gathering into clouds, falling as rain onto the Earth, flowing into streams lakes and seas, to be lifted by the winds again. Feel the energy of that great circle of the flow of water on Earth entering the circulation of your blood and purifying your whole body.

Angel of Air
Friday Morning

Angel of Air, enter my lungs and give the Air of Life to my whole body.
Imagine yourself walking in the countryside in summer, with a gentle, flowery breeze lifting your hair. As you breathe, gently become aware of the wonderful gift of Air—the Breath of Life.

The Evening Prayers
The Heavenly Father
Friday Evening

The Heavenly Father and I are One.
*Simple and profound—this statement spoken with reverence every Friday evening, will gradually allow you to understand, in the depths of your being, that you are a loved and loving part of the Great Creator, the Heavenly Father, the Law, the Light, the Supreme, the Nameless One, God.
Imagine yourself as a wave in a Great Ocean.
God is the Ocean and you are the wave.*

Angel of Eternal Life
Saturday Evening

Angel of Eternal Life, descend upon me, and give Eternal Life to my Spirit.
We ask this Great Angel to allow our Souls to fly free from the negative thoughts of earth, and reach up to the higher vibrations of Heaven.

Imagine yourself as a great flowing wind swirling around in the high mountains, leaving all negativity behind.

Angel of Creative Work
Sunday Evening

Angel of Creative Work, descend upon Humanity and give abundance to all Mankind.
We ask this Great Angel to help us to see all work as creative work, and therefore enjoyable!
Imagine yourself sitting in an apple orchard full of blossom and bees, reading a book of poetry. Think about the great masterpieces of art, literature, science and philosophy and allow their sublime energies to flow into you.

Angel of Peace
Monday Evening

Peace, Peace, Peace, Angel of Peace be always everywhere.
We ask this Great Angel to bring to your innermost self a deep and profound peace—for it is only when peace is deep within each of us, that we can create peace in the World around us.
Imagine yourself sitting beside the calm waters of a cool lake at evening. The moon is rising slowly, reflecting her peaceful light on the shining waters beside you. Allow this peace to flow into your innermost being.

Angel of Power
Tuesday Evening

Angel of Power, descend upon me and direct all my acts.

*This Great Angel will help you to absorb the Heavenly energies of the
Stars and Planets through your nervous system.
Imagine yourself lying on your back in a meadow on a warm
Summer's night, gazing at the black velvet sky,
glittering with stars.
Allow the shining energies of the Stars to flow into you.*

Angel of Love
Wednesday Evening

Angel of Love, descend upon me and purify all my feelings.
*This Great angel will show you how to see with the eyes of an Angel—
to love and honour equally, every life form on Earth and in Heaven with
pure, unconditional love.
Imagine you are gazing at a perfect rose, with pure love for its incredible, delicate beauty, its divine perfume and its hidden strength—your
love is undemanding, simple and complete. The rose is gazing at you with
pure love, undemanding, simple and complete.*

Angel of Wisdom
Thursday Evening

Angel of Wisdom, descend upon me and enlighten all my thoughts.
*Ask this Great Angel to help you to think powerful, positive thoughts.
Imagine yourself in the hush of a great library full of books of wisdom.
Allow your own inner wisdom to rise to the surface of your mind, and
blend with the Wisdom of the Ages on these shining shelves.*

THE MASTERS

Many of us are now on the path of self-realisation and self-mastery. The Solar Lords and the Hierarchy help us move forward at our own pace to reach our Christed self. Masters are those who surround you with the full glory of the Divine Light of Life, Love and Wisdom; and by surrounding you thus, aid you in your understanding.

THE TRAVELLER RETURNS

The traveller returns
Fixed in the positive elements,
A constant Star,
A light for troubled pilgrim
And journeying avatar.
Far from the night of shadow
Love's Angel sounds his horn:
The aspirant of long ages
Is risen and fullborn!
There is no turning back
To the shadowed entity,
But the Shining One will lighten
Earth's dark proclivity,
And with ten myriad brothers
In dazzling company
Set forth in lighted symbols
Man's map of destiny.
For whosoe'er would travel
From darkness into light
Must trim his lamp to enter
The positive Infinite,
Forever and forever
Illumining the way

> Till the lost realms of creation
> Blossom into Day
>
> *Pamela Constantine*

The Masters enfold you in the ever-present Divine Light of Life, Love and Wisdom, which is theirs to send out and to give. They see you always enfolded in this Omnipresent Divine Presence. They see you seated on your throne as a true king or queen, ruling through and by this Divine Presence. They envisage you knowing and accomplishing your Divine Mission, always alive, always peaceful and happy, always the Divine you. They see not only you, but the whole human family, divine and pure, and every created thing or form as divine; not one, nor one sect, nor one creed, but all and that all inclusive.

None can appreciate these great people, save those who have been admitted to the quiet of their sacred places and thoughts. They live Truth, which is part of the Universe itself. To our human self, life is bound about by every limitation and convention. To them, life is a boundless, ceaseless journey of unending bliss and happiness. They believed the longer the span of life, the greater the joy and the more worthwhile the living.

The main object of their being is to give knowledge and enlightenment to humanity through pure knowledge, aflame with love. Their great mission is to pave the way toward peace and harmony through man's great power to accomplish.

The idea of death is foreign to the divine purpose and is not in accord with the law of the Cosmos, nor its vibrant radiations. Once we have achieved true solar awakening, we will not die, just arise and fall through our own spiral at will.

There is only one Mastery to be sought, and that is over one's own outer self. The more attention you give your body, the more it is the master, and the more it will demand and keep demanding from you.

You might walk beside a Master for years and not discover it, until your own inner self reveals it. You might live with one and not know it! For a Master to discuss or disclose his own attainment of Mastery, would be to dissipate his own forces, and is not advisable. Remember, a true Master will never tell you he or she is one!

There is a mighty difference between their Divine Compassion and our human sympathy. It is as great as that between Light and darkness. Divine Compassion holds our attention anchored to the mighty I Am presence calling it forth to produce Perfection. Human sympathy is a rushing forth of energy, qualified by a feeling of imperfection, which intensifies the imperfection manifesting.

Self Mastery is possible once we consistently use the qualities of our higher nature. We do not continue to come and go into our lower and higher nature. We are steadfast in our higher positioning knowing the journey was never for the one alone, but to help humanity fly to their freedom and greater self.

Here is a list of some of the masters that have spoken in the channellings:

Kuthumi	Master for Healers
Hilarion	Master for Elevating the Spirit
Sanat Kumara	Solar Logos, Master of Many Masters
St. Germain	Overseer of the Aquarian Age
Akhenaten	Assists Self Mastery
Serapis Bey	Assists Ascension
Christ	Risen Jesus is Sananda
Mother Mary	Fosters the feminine qualities
St Francis	Serves all planetary life forms
Yogananda	Avatar of Love
Himalayan	Master of Self Realisation
Metatron	Joiner of Universal Concepts
Jupiter	Solar Master
El Morya	Master of Willpower
Maitreya	Teacher of Self Realisation
Buddha	Master of Enlightenment
Makimsih	Solar Lord
Mithunam	Overseer to see us to the Light

HEAVEN

At one time, man was fully conscious that he was the motivating center, and lived fully conscious of his inheritance and dominion. Man lived consciously in a condition that we term heaven. All but a few have let go of this divine gift, and today the great majority are absolutely unconscious of this divine quality which is mankind's true inheritance.

What man has done once, he can accomplish again.

THE VIOLET FLAME

Saint Germain, the Ascended Master, has asked us to work with the I Am principle and the Violet Flame. When we ask for the Violet Flame and visualise it, purification takes place to the level we will allow.

You can visualise a problem or a relationship in the Violet flame outside us. This should help release any difficulties. You can immerse yourself in a large Violet Flame and repeat "I Am the Violet Flame," which connects your mighty I Am presence to the Violet Flame.

Use the Violet Flame to transmute dense energies around you, and visualise the colour violet, flowing through any negative area or dense energy. This will help cleanse your auric field.

I AM AFFIRMATIONS

- **For purification, harmony and absent healing**
I Am the eternal, harmonising Presence and activity everywhere I move, and of everything to which my thought is directed

- **For a joyous, calm attitude regardless of anything that takes place**
I Am the presence which nothing can disturb

- **For destructive suggestions or bad atmospheres**
  I Am invincibly protected against any imperfect suggestion

- **To build perfection**
  I Am the Ascended Presence, I do accept the full activity of my Mighty I Am Presence

- **When irritated**
  I command through the I Am Presence that this be governed harmoniously

- **To shut out interference of the outer mind**
  I Am the Presence of Divine Love at all times

- **To fix attention on the Perfection of body when ill**
  The I Am Presence governs this physical body completely and compels it into obedience

STEPS TO SELF MASTERY

- Focus on remaining youthful
- Get enough sleep
- Maintain unconditional love for all life
- Get out of any soul-destroying job
- Cancel all negative thoughts
- Do not wallow in criticism and judgement
- Eat the right food for your body
- Choose friends wisely
- Create beauty all about you

CHAPTER NINE

REMAINING YOUTHFUL

DAILY MEDITATION

My subconscious is now continuously immersed in golden light and responds always to my true positive cheerful instructions.
It reacts only to my true positive cheerful instructions.
It cancels all else.
It is becoming part of my risen reality, which is entering heaven on earth.
Always and forever my subconscious and my true self work now as one.
I instruct my subconscious to refine and renew my human form continuously.
My subconscious is refining and renewing my human form continuously.
My subconscious helps me feel this joyous truth—my human form is constantly refined and renewed.
My subconscious leaps ahead to fulfill every one of my cheerful positive instructions, commands and suggestions.
Every day and in every way I feel younger, every day and in every way I look younger, every day and in every way I am stabilising as myself, at seventeen again, permanently.

I feel myself again, I look myself again, I feel myself at 17 again, and know this as my abiding reality, perfect form, perfect appearance, perfect functional capabilities, perfect young mind, young heart, young lungs, young shape.

I live in perfect beauty, I am completely myself at seventeen with the enduring benefit of experience.

I feel perfectly healthy—all my senses are keen and perfect, excellent eyesight, excellent hearing, perfect co-ordination, I move with pleasurable ease.

I feel fully alive again, I feel bright, strong, wise, energy filled, I am highly creative.

My feelings are always lovingly constructed. Always and forever my subconscious and my true self work now as one.

I now live in the light of my true being, I am happy again, and I am at peace again.

All is right in my world. I am eager to tackle everything with my creative zeal.

I am in perfect self harmony, I am joyful in my being, I am carefree in my life. I am efficient in all my undertakings.

I am a perfected soul in a perfected body.

I can live again in complete inner balance and enjoy being my true self as I was at seventeen with the additional benefit of experience. I am in constant renewal.

I am in constant refinement. I am in true constancy of being.

I possess complete clarity of understanding, my mind is clear and sharp, my responses are quick and calm, my actions are efficient and graceful, always and forever my subconscious and my true self work as one.

I live now in the sunlight of my true being continuously.

I live in and for heaven on earth.

I am always strong and fit. I am always true natural love, in action.

I live in and for steadfast soul love. Always and forever my
subconscious and my true self work as one.
I am constantly being created into further light, and beauty, further
strength and well being.
I am a natural unit of the new heaven on the new earth.
I am fulfilling my heavenly blueprint right now and always. Every day
I bring more beauty into manifestation.
Every day I express more beauty, for I am a being
created from beauty.
Every day I grow more wonderfully creative, for I am a being created
from wonder.
Every day I bring more love into my life.
Every day I give more love.
Every day I grow more lovingly expressive, for I am a being created
from love.
Every day I draw forth more wisdom.
Every day I share more wisdom, for I am a being created from
wisdom.
I am fitter now than ever.
I look better now than ever.
I am younger now than ever.
I look younger now than ever.
I am stronger now than ever.
I am truly being forever in my springtime, and always and forever my
subconscious and my true self
work as one, always and forever.
Transformation is now occurring to me fully
and completely from within.
My subconscious is now permanently at one with my true eternal
character and all will come out all right.
I accept this now throughout my being.
All is now in beneficial motion.

Remember that youth is God's seed of love planted in the human form divine. Indeed, youth is the divinity within man; youth is the life spiritual—the life beautiful. It is only life that lives and loves—the one life eternal. Age is unspiritual, mortal, ugly and unreal. Fear thoughts, pain thoughts and grief thoughts create the ugliness called old age. Joyous thoughts, love thoughts, and ideal thoughts create the beauty called youth. Age is but a shell within where lays the gem of reality—the jewel of youth.

Practice acquiring the consciousness of childhood, and visualise the Divine Child within. Before falling asleep suggest to your subconscious:

I now realise that there is within me a spiritual joy-body,
ever young, ever beautiful.
I have a beautiful, spiritual mind, eyes, nose, mouth and skin—the
body of the Divine Infant, which now tonight, is perfect.

Repeat this affirmation and meditate upon it quietly whilst falling asleep. Upon rising in the morning suggest to yourself aloud:

Well dear (*your name*) there is a divine alchemist within.

By the spiritual power of these affirmations during the night, a transmutation takes place and the unfolding from within the spirit has saturated your being. The inner alchemist has caused dead and worn out cells to fall away, and the gold of new skin to appear with perpetual health and loveliness. Truly, divine Love in demonstration is eternal youth.

Also, learn to smile in the sweet way of a child. A smile from the soul is spiritual relaxation. A real smile is a thing of true beauty, the artistic work of the Inner Ruler Immortal. Affirm:

I think a kind thought for all the world.
May all the world be happy and blessed.

Before you go to work you can affirm:

Within me there is a perfect form—the form Divine.
I am now all that I desire to be!

> I visualise daily my beautiful being until
> I breathe it into expression!
> I am a Divine Child, all my needs are being
> Now, and forever supplied.

Make everything bright and beautiful about you. Cultivate a spirit of humour and affirm:
> **Infinite Love fills my mind and thrills my body
> with its perfect life.**

Chapter Ten

The Many Aspects of Soul

When we tune into soul awareness fragments lost start to re-appear, and all slots into place. We have not really lost anything. We have just regained our vision. We look over the horizon being wide-awake to all possibilities and all ways to being true to our soul.

We could be climbing Mount Everest and giving healing on another planet. We could be writing love poems, or helping sick children in the many characters we can create from our soul. We can be a nun, a monk, a saint, an artist, an author; anything we choose, all at the same time. Masters say we can do one thousand different things at the same moment.

Our soul, in waking up, answers all our human questions. To step back into soul again is beyond any words in our vocabulary. During our final stages of enlightenment and awakening, we need to receive silent healing to reach the last furlong Home.

We are limited in the body, but in soul we can look after many people, yet love everyone as though they are the only one. It is being a part of the Universal Christos. It is the future for all, to reach these heights.

Soul is a state of being—the essential state. It can manifest if it wants, or not. It is of itself pure, and in the essential state we are capable of working on all sorts of vibrations at the same time. Think of oneself as a range of vibrant energies issuing from the Self. Spirit can come to many at the same time, and work at the same time. We will have this ability. It is a letting go of limiting concepts, and beyond rational thought.

What is Earth? Earth is a planet, and because soul has manifested itself in a physical body, we think we are living on the earth as a human soul. Unknown to our human soul in its earthly exterior, we may be working on Jupiter, Mars, or elsewhere, in another set of frequencies from our soul. And even then we do not have to be in such limitation as we are now. When working in these other realms we are no longer in a totally dense physical nature, yet work on an etheric level. So on a different level of our being, we could be working there fully employed doing spiritual work. So this idea that earth is a place, or heaven is a place, is not true. All is a state of our soul. Our soul is our home, our base, and we can go off in all kinds of directions and appear in any aspect. So, where we appear we seem to be alive, but in soul we are fully alive. So when we come home to our soul, all of this is real to us.

This will take us time because we are used to this idea of having a physical form. Our form is not as physical as we think. Form is a set of energy points all pulsating at the same rate. Physicists know this, and this is the only reason that we see ourselves as a solid mass. Physical form is a mass of condensed energy pulsating at the same rate, which our brain perceives as solid. So when our vibration is quickened, the energies rise and by rising they become invisible to the human eye, but visible to Spirit. And this is how you are able to visit your higher self.

You can then be brought back to your normal rate of vibration at which time you are visible again. So you see, what a joke the idea of physicality and being rooted in time really is. The idea of time is getting to be an outdated idea. Many people are grasping that we do not belong in this physical mass, and we can move rapidly to, and do more in the higher frequencies. We have a habit of conditional thinking and following each other's patterning. We think in terms of physicality and time, which we need to eliminate to move forward.

July 1998
Dr. Kruger

It dawns on you, as you get closer, until you have one little understanding waiting, and at that moment there you are. It is a temporary situation while you try little ways of perceiving what is going on. Because you are changing so rapidly within, and all this is taking up energies, altering rhythms, adjusting the physical all the time, because it is under new management, the higher self is now within the cortex of the scalp. This means directions are direct and absolute. They are instinctive, so they do not need a voice, or brain to unravel them. You have to let go of the brain in this activity. The soul mind is beginning to glow and to know.

You will have easy access to people, and won't be bothered about buying a bus ticket, or jumping in a car; you will be flying through from one place to the next to see what you can do to help. You have a busy life ahead.

You will get your dues when you come Home. All your efforts will reap its benefits. We acknowledge your work. We know what you are doing. We appreciate you very much, and you will know all about that when you meet us. This is a delightful time for us all.

Now that you are getting close to the enlightened state, I can step further towards you. It is not all done by question and answer, no matter what your schoolteachers tell you. This is a higher matter we are thinking of.

You will be questioning, "who am I," until you get through the gate, and then you know "this is who I am". You are always just you, what you were, and what you might have been does not count here. What you have made yourself that is what counts. The soul is your potential being. You can take anything you want from the soul—it is all there. No matter who you are. Qualities and attributes you need are all in the soul, so when a life comes along you say "I take this, that and that and that, so I'll be this part of my soul, for this part of the journey".

So now you see when you are coming Home you are all that potential and you become aware of it and you can say "Well, I think I'd like to help in that area, so I take this, this, this, and I draw upon all my resources from my experiences, and

I will be a completely useful person for that work". Do you see? So you can be many coming out from the soul center, all very different from one another, but at source you are yourself.

You are working in many different layers and different capacities really, then you are visible to the people you help in different ways. It would be very confusing because one would say, Lady Jayne visited me last night, and another would say no, she visited me. She wasn't like that she was like this, so you have it wrong. That is why they have different names and different appearances.

Your three-dimensional world likes everything in black and white, but there are many colours in spirit. There is also a deeper area of ourselves where we do not need language, and when you come Home you will find that when you are in soul, you do not need language. Everything is understood, and those in soul too will understand you. There is no need of language instead you exchange Light.

Light is the Love Intelligence. When you see Lights fleeting about what we are doing, we are communicating. It is silent exchange. Always true of soul 'level', we do not think of levels. We think of the entire Universe being the one Universe of Love, and we do not make divisions, dimensions as souls, but because you are slowly coming Home, we help you by coming in those layers you perceive as steps. So this is why people from spirit will sometimes say there is no separation here—we are all in one world. And others say, "No, there are dimensions or levels". It depends where spirit is coming from as much as you.

If we want to transform down to reach you, then we do that. Then you access us, and we seem to be at a particular level or in a particular dimension of ourselves, but you are now coming all the way Home to the soul centre. No dimensions or levels exist. You just take up the right position for the person you want to meet. It is simple when you are here. Once you've got Home, it is very clear, and know not to judge the different explanations.

Practice connecting with your higher self and the explanations will flow. It doesn't matter then who gives the information, it will be the same. We are all together in the higher.

Here there is no need for hot baths, brushing your teeth, getting in the car. We are in appearance only. We are solid to those who wish it, of course. There is a lot of magic waiting. To the physical mind, everything is either this or that. It cannot be both. Here, it can. Expect wonders, miracles—to us these are commonplace, but we adore them. It is an extraordinary life; and where you live right now must seem very ordinary as you get nearer to us......

Marcus Aurelius Antoninus
"Get rid of the judgment; you are rid of the 'I am hurt'; get rid of the 'I am hurt', you are rid of the hurt itself".
from MEDITATIONS by Marcus Aurelius (AD121-180)

This is different—I have come to my true self long ago and I elected to go on serving through my last known appearance for as long as it took some of you to travel upwards. Well, you are travelling so well that I feel it is the time to come to you from my advanced level of being. So today, I am also to be known to you as Antoninus. I have a past in that name, but today I use it to demonstrate that I carry with me the philosophic approach to life that I developed in that span.

It has helped the old Kruger, and helped others too who have been my patients and my pupils. I am so happy to be sharing with you, Jayne, for here I lose my accent and come into my own. I am already discernible as part of the counterpart here. People tend to think of us in spirit the same as the people on earth—they merely think they have moved on and they are learning more, so they are more advanced. Yes, but so much more is involved.

When on earth, you are usually just a small aspect of your wholeness, but it all comes together before ascension, for you and your group that you are in. That is why I wanted to come on this finer level, because I have information, because I have done it. I can go up and down, and I can remain with the surname of Kruger, but it is a measure of your advancements that I now release my name in spirit.

I kept my name Antoninus because I was proud of my achievement in that life. It is to me perhaps the highest that the human brain can accomplish, that is the level of the philosopher. After that, you are not any longer using the human brain. When you are graduating through the chakra levels to become more the mystic, then you are utilising some of the higher self-mind. So you see as a philosopher, I am standing my ground just below clarity vibration to help you to establish more therein. I give you my helping hand, and I am happy to keep you company for the rest of this interesting journey.

While I am in this capacity, as someone who likes a discussion on the way life is, is there anything you wish to lay before me today?

Jayne: "Have I finished my karma?"

All you have left now is what I believe is instant karma. Even that can be dismissed, for we are not judges any more than you are of others. All are allowed to gauge for themselves how they want to adjust themselves to move on—it is never a matter of applying rules from outside. It is an inner matter. So as long as you feel right with a thing, it is right for you. As for making up for past mistakes, I would say they are past. Why bother with them? If you are concerned for people you think you might have wronged, I would say those people are also past. I am not trying to make people become undisciplined. They should all feel right with themselves and the journey, for as long as you are on, it helps you do this more and more. It should not be looked at a series of hardships, trials and tests. It is only that you are gradually adjusting until you are right with yourself, and so with life.

You are in a human form, and the human form carries inherently a subconscious. In that subconscious layer of memory, sometimes for various reasons, can cause that memory to return. You relive it but there is no need to. It is like the life of a ghost. It is not really any more. It only has the power that you give to it. So let it go without recrimination to it, or yourself. Accept that that is part of the human condition. If anybody should tell you that they have nothing from the past bothering them, that they have found a way, that it will never happen to them again, I guarantee that they will eat their words in time to come, until that is, they have re-birthed. Then it is true there is no longer the human subconscious to be dealt with. You are in what you call superconscious. Everything is clear and plain and straightforward, so you don't harbour doubts and anxiety, as you are prone to do when you carry this memory box around. But anything that you have learnt that is worthwhile is, of course, part of your soul's structure because your soul has fed on it and so you are that very being. You have gleaned all the good you can and now you are ready to bring it home to us where you enrich us with what you have learnt. So it is a two-way mutual benefit. We help you, and you indeed help us.

Jayne: *"Is our higher self the same as our soul?"*

It is a matter of where you are standing when you look at it. I mean by this it is a matter of perspective. Each person, has their own ideas on the matter. I would say go by what it feels like to you because it is your way of understanding the terms. Do go by your own understanding of things. This becomes more and more important. One of my chief delights is meeting with other philosophers, and others who have had similar experiences while on earth, who are now here with me. We can share these matters, and I will say my understanding is thus and another will say, that is interesting, my understanding is like this. And we learn from each other. If we all saw it exactly the same there would be nothing to discuss. There would be no room for individual perspectives. We need individuality for as long as I can see into eternity. So worry not if you are puzzled by certain terms. Try your own understanding out until it satisfies you. That is my best advice.

Jayne: *"I feel I would like to be with the younger ones."*

You are now very close to soul awareness and the soul so yearns that younger generations will not have your struggle to awaken your soul. So the desire is to touch as many of the young as is possible. For this reason because you are closer to the soul awareness now this urge is becoming more conscious. And so, what the soul desires is always granted by the Great Creative Spirit. You may be surprised at the direction the answer arrives in flesh and blood.

Well, this has been most pleasurable. You will get used to me here—you may look me up. I am in history as Antoninus. You will see why I seem very composed and at peace with myself. It was a good life in which I did peak spiritually and I am happy to utilise that now for you. My blessings. I hope to be back in a similar vein.

God bless you. Thank you.

Chapter Eleven

Special Moments

April 1997
SOLAR LOGOS

Through the power of the Solar Logos we greet you today with a deep joy and peace. For we are agreed with that which you perceive as the right route, forward. We are naturally aware of the many difficulties of living in a human world with all its materialistic problems, but we are also working to bring about a satisfactory arrangement whereby you are fully released to do that which your soul desires to accomplish. For we, of course, recognise it is all for the sake of Love. This too being our purpose, we now move forward in perfect unity. Receive therefore our energy from the divine in its sweetest most natural form, our essential self-powers. Know thou this, because it is thy wish and it is thy will, it is that of ourselves of which you speak. Thus joint as one, thee and us, the power will be there for that which is to be.

April 1997
SAINT GERMAIN

I am the brother Germain. I rejoice to come to you, for behold, my time has come. My ideas, my inspiration is gradually infiltrating my beloved group. I have overwatched your lives as separate entities, and I have gently and unobtrusively brought you closer into contact in your every day lives, so that the plan I held in mind so long ago might at last, in my Age of Aquarius, come into fulfillment.

Each of you has several gifts that you have been burnishing. You have a sense of their purport. You understand the nature of the times, that the Aquarian Age is that period whereby humanity moves into the light of the perennial age, liberated as an immortal once more. I am filled with the fire of enthusiasm as I greet you. I have been banking up the fires. I have been busy intensifying my connection with each one of you through your soul twins, and through your illuminators and other inspirers. I have even managed to communicate my intentions through the feelings in those who are in your world, but not yet aware. In turn, their works have acted to spark off ideas for some of you.

Beloved daughter of Sharkti, I hold in my hands the pitcher of consciousness, and the libation I pour over thy spiritual head now is that which encloaks thee as an illuminant of Sharkti. Our continent is just into the sublime where our beloveds meet, congregate and exchange their plans for assisting humanity through this epoch. Loved ones from many dimensions also gather here today to provide the intense love, which is need for you to feel first. Then from this feeling of cherishment, from this sense of being cared for and loved by all of us, you will be enabled to free the waiting Self into expression, enfranchised, distinct, and unique.

The long wait is nearly over when the pent up creative spirit, housed in flesh, will again speak with the tongues of Angels, will express to the lyre of the Muse, will begin all over again to re-introduce those beauteous waves of spiritual artistry that come down through the planes from Sharkti to common earth. Yet, when you begin to wake, when even through your expressions you yourselves grow wise, you will see the earth differently. Some will call it a risen earth, but it is your awareness that has risen. For I too am entering the heart chakra, to touch and enliven once again the weary spirit on mission on your earth. Soon my libation over each one of your spiritual heads will quicken the insight, the soul's memory, and things will begin to germinate.

New seeds will flourish, and although we are not in embodiment know the problems you face in your straight jacketed world where laws are not always in the interest of the society they are meant to serve. Yet, we ourselves will be instrumental in changing things appropriately. We are coming together in the next higher plane from your earth....

October 1997
TED FLOODGATE

Hello, my dear, Eduardo here. Well I'm a guy that likes to shake the hand, you know. Nice to meet you! A long while since I was on the earth, you know, but then you would have been about so high, but not all that long ago.

This has been quite a day for us. Always we are pleased to come. But today you may have noticed time has slowed down a little. We could do more in a more relaxed way. As you awaken you will find this more, it is like time is expanding and fading out of mind. You will find the going easier, my dear. This is where as the mind expands and the feelings respond, you are beginning to access what you are like on the more etheric levels. It is good. For as you know the brother Dr. Kruger has been working on the quickening of the higher chakras to make this as comfortable as possible. Now you are reaping a little of the benefits.

Jayne: *"I'm still shaking though!"* (I had shudders in my body for at least six months, especially when I felt the guide's presence.)

Well, perhaps you can see how different it would be if it had been a mortal transition. Therefore, be glad. It is a sign. It is a good sign, and once the brain knows you are satisfied it will not have an adverse effect. It is good to know these things. Well, my dear, I've got to be going, but very pleased to make your acquaintance in a deeper way today. As you have noticed no contact needed, meeting as people do, face to face. It is far better. It will come. The day will also come when we are open eyed. This will be so. Once you feel comfortable we will do that. That is the precursor of the time when we will stand before you ourselves. So little by little, you are practising for that moment and so are we. Well, m'dear, God bless you. Hope to return on another occasion. Cheerio my dear.

October 1997
TUTANKHAMEN

For long centuries I have awaited this time of my earthly renewal through the lips of others, through the understanding of other's hearts. I come forth from the tomb revitalised, renewed to speak again. For I was entombed before death, but I have arisen and am awake, and now understand myself. So I come as a servant for a new time for humanity. I come with jewels and gifts, but they are not of earth. I wish to comment that many like me, who stand out from history, are not truly recorded. Because of this we return to put matters straight, and also to be of greater use this time around. I remember when I was able to assist my people, but I thought narrowly of the Egyptians. Now I see that all are family. I am eager to play my part. I wish not to write in hieroglyphics, but to warm the human heart to understand. So I come bearing gifts of love. I bow the knee, and thank you for receiving me. Tutankhamen.

October 1997
AZRAELLA

Azraella here, I am moving gently in the spiral with you, enfolding you in my wings, helping you feel the rhythm with your twin partner, Helping you know it is he who establishes the deepest rapport,
Helping you know it is him who will help you write the score,
Helping you know it is him who will love you forever more.
Azraella here, Azraella there, always with you now and ever more.

November 1997
LILY FLOODGATE

Hello, hello, hello, Lily, Lily, Lily. I'm coming in ever so fast now, and ever so strong to help you with all your patients more. They told me I was the one, so here I am. I want to work to the full, you see, and there is always more energy whatever I seem to do. So here I am. I am coming with you wherever you go where there is need of healing. Thank you. Lily, Lily, Lily.

December 1997
JUPITER

We of Jupiter welcome thee. For often now you transport to us, and we give you of our knowingness. We bring you signs of future achievement that will be yours. For we have already come to our selves as flames of light. We wish to be impartial embodiments in order to work between the worlds. As I speak, as a woman of the solar etheric planes of the beloved Jupiter, I am lifting your flame to be parallel to my own. To show you and let you feel how it is when the flame has risen and is still, but it inhabits a form.

It is quiet, it is restful, it is fully conscious of its source in love, and so it gravitates to darkened areas where it can throw some light, where it can feed the starving ones, and this also your heart yearns to do.

And thus, it was deemed fit that you should come to us and practice for a while the raising of the flame to the extent that we have here. Our people are some ten or twelve feet tall but the flame that they are raises another foot and a half above their heads. This flame is still at all times. No matter how we move, whether fast or slow, whether we circle, whether we are still, that flame never falters. It is always completely itself, and our children are still learning that placidity. It is because of this their little flames flow wide away whenever they are pulled in a certain direction. They learn to be stabilised flames just like us.

So there are many ways of being, but to be at peace in the heart is to bring together all aspects in harmony. We, are a harmonious citizenry.

We come to share our feelings. We come to bring you that which has helped us, and we give you our gift of love for the time ahead when that gift will be called upon in many different ways. It will be your pleasure to give again that gift according to your judgement. It shall be so.

Keep then those tapes of which we convey the future for your own purpose, but also, that these things that demonstrate what were your needs at those times can be of service to others.

Our love is instant, direct, fully conscious, and we merge with yours in certain activities of rescue and healing. Therefore, we are as brothers and sisters of the divine light in thee. As then thy brothers and sisters, we give you our Christmas wishes for on your plane this is that time for the celebration of the Christ light, and we love to honour it, too. Our warmest blessings that the flame may reach to the fullest extent and, being at home, achieve all things. Salutations.

December 1997
THE AMORATAS

Where once we used to tutor the flame
Where once we used to guide
Now you have caught your own rhythmic pulse
And we are at your side.
We watch, we wait and never yet have needed to interfere
For you are taking all right steps and we applaud our peer.
We watch, we move, even as you, to a higher destiny.
Beloved one the goal awaits and the best is yet to be,
Then all the lives that went before are simply slaked away
And love distils from all of them love alone will stay
And as I speak the counterpart draws very closely in
Whispering words beyond all hearing to his enchanted twin
You will receive further communication from him direct
Soul to soul, by this you will proceed.
As he approaches in reality, of us you will have no need
Yet even so we are at hand, you only have to ask,
Meanwhile, I simply come to thee appreciating thy task,
For it seems long but is quite short and others follow through,
Leaving the joyous way of ways to thy twin soul and you.
Be unafraid the rest is light, for the load is thrown off soon,
And you will know the joy of life, you will know what I know now
And cannot even find a rhyme for!
Beloved, my life is full of laughter for I am happy now.
Who toiled and laboured while on earth, is beyond the shining plough.

I am no longer using the plough to plant the heavenly seed
For when there are such souls as thou whatever is the need?
Open to the high impress, you come at last to us,
And yet already are making plans to fly the incubus.
And so you will and so you are, how very glad are we.
For in accepting your true role you are setting others free.
Because of this I come with deepest thanks to thee.

January 1998
CLARA BUTT

I am Clara Butt. My warm greetings to you! I managed to achieve a career through my voice, and you are now giving us a voice. But voices will fade as your own will takes precedence, then you will have all the wisdom on tap. It will be your own and yours to share as you will. We have kept company through this your present life, an amazing array of us, I might say, and we have been most happy to be there for thee. As I speak, members of the higher choir already prepare for you a welcome song into your full stature of being once more. For as you come into the consciousness of Self, so long awaited, you will have and hold all the knowledge and wisdom of the ages, but according to your own direct insights. It is this that is of the profoundest value to us. Indeed to others that will seek you out in the time not too advanced from now.

We have mentioned on occasion, that you will write another book(!) Although this seems unlikely, yet so it is, but this will give you much more satisfaction. It will be the one you will want to write for yourself, and it will equip many to have a greater understanding of how heaven and earth are married in the individual. For that is the step your humanity is learning to take. No wonder there seems many pitfalls. No wonder many stumble. But in them is the inexorable voice urging them to awaken now. For the soul of humanity has been stirred, and will no longer continue its slumber. Some will be slow to fully awaken, but many will be eager, and some of these you will help along the way.

This book then will become their travelling companion, freeing you to the glorious art world that awaits. My brother Holbein extends his welcome. He smiles, for he sees the affinity right well. Also, the brothers Turner and Constable. They are drawn in now. For indeed by your manner of awakening, you provide for these a further way of reaching the human being in need. Therefore, we the entire company, thank thee. Thy friend Clara.

January 1998
FRANCIS BACON

Francis Bacon here. It is good indeed to see one so dedicated pursuing her true life line. I had to hide my identity throughout my human life in order to put over what I had to come to say. You are living in a more enlightened age. True, it has only just started, but you will live to see a fuller blossoming of the Aquarian Age, and through it my works will give way to newcomers like yourself who have something fresh to say in a more modern idiom, but in accordance with their individuality. This thrills me. It means I can finally give up my post and move forward. I am in that of Germain, but I always have a foot on your earth. So many remember the Shakespeare, yet as that phase and the new creators begin to make their mark, this will release me further, and so in advance I wish to convey my thanks for the part you will play. Not with deliberate intent, but because it is in your heart to do that very thing. My felicitations and gratitude to you. Thank you, thank you, thank you!

January 1998
BEYOND THE SOLAR

Then from beyond even the solar, we who rarely come to words whisper our love to thee. We who for many aeons have been free and awake and aware, who draw about the mind of the Godhead, stretch forth in radius, to thee today, beaming the love of divinity. Lifting the spirit, we understand all the stages, we merge as you rise, and are part of the elevation. We move in intense vibrance of peace. Our movements are solar, but our beings are beyond shape. Moving at will, we touch into human fabric bringing forth an illumination of thought or feeling. We are nameless save that we are love. Stemming from that bright nimbus of power we seek those who are learning to be steadfast in spirit, that we may absorb the last of their shadow, and enable them to step up and amplify their own light. We were called, and we came. You are being called, and gradually response will come. Life will not be then as now you know it, for as you step into the solar field you will be amazed at your own self recognition, and recognition of those who have loved you endlessly from beyond time, and even sometimes through it. You are as that sun, waiting to lift to its zenith, to reach out its' twinfold rays, and enter other darkened virginal lands. Peace is our make-up. Vibration is our vehicle. Love is our all. Thus, we come to thee this day with the multitudinous blessings of the most-high God.

Receive and be still again, knowing you are worthy and almost ready for the great upsurgence that will give you back to yourself as you are in reality. Once achieved, you will never turn back, but from that brightness touch so many in shadow, and that same beauty of light will beckon to them, bringing them out of the caves and caverns into the fullness of their own beings. Only lighted love can achieve this. Therefore, we are with you to the very end to the illusion you call time. We are the nameless who love, and we are with thee.

January 1998
MARIO LANZA

Mario Lanza: Bless you for being where I could come and say my words. I would sing them, but I think perhaps I should speak. I love the atmosphere here. I have grown to my full estate, but I still love to sing. But when I need to I whisper to little children in their sleep to give them an idea of the harmony, of the melody of life. I am a close contact in your team. I asked long ago when I saw your talents, and I remain very pleased to have been accepted. My own heart is full of jubilance now, and when I see you stricken low I come and hum and sing to you to help lift the spirit. I feel for you.

I was a little bit temperamental myself, but I learnt of my steadfast side when I got Home. As you are getting Home, you will find you can do this more readily. I am very pleased I have the chance to give a little sign here and there.

I was amongst those who cleared the feelings today. We are not all doctors! We are some of us performers like thee. But you now, I believe, will be going to a nicer phase where your creativity is the main function, and others do the rest. That is what we are trying to bring about, and also for the lady here (Pam), *because you are both going to do much more by being creative spirits in form. We delight you are there, and we delight to be there sometimes too. I have grown up in spirit for I was rather mixed up, you know, but now I have what you say have got it together, and I am a happy individual now. When I can I will get back to you. When you are very still perhaps you will hear me singing again. Till then next we speak, Mario…*

April 1998
SIRIUS

I, Sirius, have waited silently until this moment where feelings can be ignited in a solar manner. In reaching to earth, I begin to convey the profound emotion of the solar masculine world. In you is the complementary emotional vibrationary field, and as I attune to it I am overjoyed with what you have already accomplished. I now live in the heights of my being as you are coming to do. As this takes place over a quiet stage of growth, your emotions will change and be so positive and relaxed, you will never again need to descend to the sorrows and despairs of the past. Even if there is a departure of loved relatives in future times yet in your solar stronghold you will find such a different response—a joy response for those loved and liberated from the physical difficulties. You are beginning to shine like an evening star, and we of the inner constellations of light respond to you. Be still often, beloved soul sister Jayne, and you will get to know us all over again, consciously and in your emotions too.…

June 1998
REMBRANDT

I am your friend Rembrandt. Though tastes in art may differ across the years, we do have much in common. I continue to draw and paint, but my inner life is much more awake now. I see things I never thought possible for the human eye to see. But because the illumined ones have lit my heart I am able to see through, to see with my own eyes the beauty that was hidden from me when I walked your earth. So of course, in my love of beauty I could not give up my art, and I continue happily with the brush.

I look at your poor world. So much has happened to it since my time, and it troubles me that there is much that is un-beautiful. I hope when you next visit my realm in sleep state we may talk about this, and perhaps it might even help you to bring forth something very beautiful, but different from what went before. There is nothing like first hand contact, so I hope this will be arranged when your dear twin flame takes you off by night. Your friend Rembrandt.

June 1998
SANAT KUMARA

Sanat Kumara. More and more I visit with my light. You have already known me as the Solar Logos of your planet. Now once more I come close. I bring down my light for all children of earth. No little one shall ever be without conscious light again when the Age of Aquarius is complete. You are establishing in your own light now. I will help you, and you will return to us in your higher dress and then you will know how you will proceed, but with utmost joy. My light I lend to companion yours.

September 1998
THUNDERCLOUD

As now we raise thy spirit high
To greet the final flame,
We call upon the God of Gods
We call your God by name.
Receive thou this, a holy one
Who waits to enter in.
Who has a million tasks achieved,
And no more crowns to win.

For each and all whisper "well done"
And bring thee to the fore,
That in thy love and in thy works
You accomplish even more.

I as a keeper of the higher archives come to bid thee welcome, and give thee the key to the further kingdom. Receive, receive, receive.

All is being accomplished according to thy innate design. All goeth well. We rejoice that thou art more here than ever, and will be hearing from us in a different way. This will come to pass and bring thee joy.

Thundercloud blesses the divine daughter of light.

September 1998
SOCRATES

I am Socrates. I have been elected to speak, and I am enjoying every moment of it. It is rare indeed that I am called in at such an advanced stage in a human soul's development, for it is considered that I am at my best working with the brain mind. However, this is never really so. It is just one stage of my work.

I have come close to greet you warmly, and say that I intend to walk the homeward route with you. Because I have been home, and I know the journey now and I am so very happy that I did, because it makes me more able as a servant of the light. Thank you for giving me this lovely chance to work alongside. I have brought my own lantern, and I am shining it vividly on the path. I hope it will add its own nuance to your movements. Here we are most concerned with your lighthood, with your dazzling, starlike self. That she should come to full estate, and reign thereafter over her own world. So this is where past masters of some particular spiritual art are called in.

You will notice that our way of speech is somewhat different today. It is because a wave of happiness has swept through us all as we see you both advancing quietly and surely to join us. We are eager and excited one and all, for we know what you have put into the journey, and we are always so proud to meet the homecome, after so long away. Nearer and nearer we come, and we *stretch as far as we can to clasp your hands, to shake your hands, and welcome you in. This is the final furlough I hear, and is excellent to know. We watch in uncounted millions, for this is a very self-enhancing experience, one which they may have never been privileged to witness before.*

You would be amazed if you realised how few travel all the way home and fully understand. It is a mighty journey involving every little aspect of your being. That is what makes it wonderful even to us. All of us are calling out, "well done!" Continue to approach the throne. We shall all be there to greet you with great pride and love. For the moment, I continue to serve you under the old name, Socrates.

November 1998
MARGARET

M-ar-ga-ret! M-ar-ga-ret! I like my name, I do. Do you like yours, Aunty? I think it is because it is for a purpose. I don't know why I got a Margaret for a purpose, but I have. Hahaha! And mummy says I've got to learn to, what's the word mummy? I've got to discipline my laughing!

'Cos she says sometimes it gets in the way of my words, and my words are a little bit more important than my giggles, haha-ha! But I want to giggle, I do, haha. Mummy, I made her laugh. I did it, alright? Mummy says yes, it's all right. Hahaha. Ha ha ha ha. I did it, I did it!

Bye!

November 1998
FRANZ LEHAR

Blessings, kind lady of musical nature. I lived my short span on earth not very long ago. I achieved a lot, but nothing like my intention. So I whisper melodies to your inner ear. I hope you will come across them soon. I am Franz Lehar. I thank you for letting me reach back to your people, and I send the love of my composer friends, one of whom is so very close to your heart. God's greetings to you, and for now goodbye.

Chapter Twelve

Twelve Steps to Heaven

I hope the channellings in this book have inspired you as they have me. Without weekly sessions with Pam and feeling the vibration of the soul family, I would not be able to reach heavenly heights on an everyday basis. I would thoroughly recommend receiving this specific channelling for a regular amount of time to create a profound effect. If this is not possible, here are the important Twelve Steps to follow.

1. CLEAR YOUR SUBCONSCIOUS MIND   *Clarity*

You must do a lot of work to clear any negative patterns and fears held in your subconscious mind, and many useful exercises are in my book The Call of an Angel. You will probably need a good therapist, preferably a hypnotherapist or counsellor working with the subconscious.

Even though you may have done a lot of work on yourself there are still often remnants of negativity to let go of. Once you are satisfied that the work is mostly over, there is then a space for true peace, pure love, and deeper soul connection.

EXERCISE
1. **Find a quiet place with no interruptions.**
2. **Close your eyes.**

3. Ask to be surrounded by Love and Light.
4. Relax every part of your body starting at your feet, through your legs, abdomen, chest, back, arms to fingertips, neck, shoulders, face muscles and scalp.
5. To relax more deeply count from one to ten.
6. Find yourself back in the womb and attached to you as you grow is a rope. This rope represents all painful moments in your life as you tie a knot in it each time you remember a negative incident. You grow in the womb and then in life slowly until the present moment. Keep tying the knots at each appropriate point.
7. When you are finished, find some scissors to totally cut the rope away from you. Then throw it far away and set light to it with a match. Let the rope burn to ashes and see them fly away in the wind. When completed, count from ten to one then open your eyes again and say "at one I am wide awake feeling refreshed and renewed".

Repeat this exercise until there are no more knots left and your negative past has dissolved.

2. SELF-HONESTY   *UNDERSTANDING*

To be self-honest is to be aware of how you react in all circumstances. Learn how to avoid over-emotion, drama, and negative relationships. Know thyself. Know what makes you happy and keep being happy. Release all guilt about staying happy. All of these approaches will assist in your self-growth and soul awareness.

SURVEY
Answer these questions with Yes or No, honestly

1. Are you over involved with the third dimensional and the material world?
2. Do you often judge others?

3. Do you often blame others?
4. Do you often lose your temper?
5. Do you avoid listening to others?
6. Do you always follow the suggestions of others?
7. Do you seek approval and affirmation?
8. Do you fail to recognize your accomplishments?
9. Is it important to you to be in a powerful position relative to others?
10. Do you fear criticism?
11. Do you enjoy showing up people who think they are right?
12. Do you consider yourself more competitive than cooperative?
13. Are you stubborn and set in your ways?
14. Do you enjoy a good argument?
15. Are you afraid to disagree with others?
16. Do you have a need for perfection?
17. Are you uneasy when your life is going smoothly? Do you continually anticipate problems?
18. Do you feel more alive in the midst of crisis?
19. Do you have a habit of creating dramas?
20. Do you speak about spiritual values, yet not act on them?
21. Do you often live in the past?
22. Do you care for others easily yet find it difficult to care for yourself?
23. Do you isolate yourself from other people?
24. Do you respond with anxiety to authority figures and angry people?
25. Do you feel that individuals and society in general are taking advantage of you?
26. Do you have trouble with intimate relationships?
27. Do you attract and seek people who tend to be compulsive?

28. Do you cling to relationships because you are afraid of being alone?
29. Do you often mistrust your own feelings and the feelings expressed by others?
30. Do you find it difficult to express your emotions?
31. Is it difficult for you to relax and have fun?
32. Do you find yourself compulsively eating, working, drinking, using drugs, or seeking excitement?
33. Have you tried various therapies, yet still feel that something is wrong or missing?
34. Do you frequently feel numb, empty or sad?
35. Is it hard for you to trust others?
36. Do you have an over-developed sense of responsibility?
37. Do you feel a lack of fulfillment in life, both personally and in your work?
38. Do you have feelings of guilt, inadequacy or low selfesteem?
39. Do you have a tendency toward having chronic fatigue, aches and pains?
40. Do you find it difficult to visit your parents, sister or brother for more than a few minutes or a few hours?
41. Are you uncertain about how to respond when people ask about your feelings?
42. Have you been mistreated or neglected as a child?
43. Do you have difficulty asking for what you want from others?

Answers
Yes—you may need to clear these issues.
No—you are doing well.

Rising to soul awareness can often lessen the importance of these issues, but if something is still in the way of consistent soul joy—seek

help, release it, or switch the switch by substituting a negative approach by a positive one.
You are going to have to make your own mind up and be very self-honest. Be honest enough to listen to your heart and then ask, "Do I need any more help on any issues?" What is the correct therapy for me?
Nevertheless, if a bad pattern continues, you may be reluctant to see the pay off in your life for this negativity, or do not want to change through fear of the unknown or unsure what will replace the behaviour. If this is so, it is your choice but it is likely that you may stand still for a long time becoming frustrated. It could be the last thing that blocks consistent joy.
You may never reach pure soul happiness unless you let go.
Take courage, take heart and ask Dr. Kruger!

3. MEDITATION — *PEACE*

Daily meditation is a necessity for attunement to soul and for clarity. Whichever method, whether silence or with a tape it is not important. What is important is time for self and letting go into just being.

RECOMMENDED DAILY MEDITATION

1. Sit or lie in a quiet place for twenty minutes.
2. Chant the OM sound through each chakra, the seven main ones, starting with the base chakra.
3. Bring a ball of white light to your crown.
4. Bring the light down your spine through to the seven main chakras from base to crown.
5. Bring your soul flame from your body to rise from your crown into the five chakras above. Breathe light into your flame above your head.

6. Say five times each: "I am clarity", "I am Harmony and Balance", "I am Eternal Peace", "I am Divine Purpose and Joy", "I am Transforming".
7. Remain in stillness for twenty minutes.

4. RECEIVE HEALING　　　　*PURIFICATION*

Receiving healing on a weekly basis is highly recommended for attunement to your soul. This is the best and quickest way to link with your own wisdom and guidance from your soul family. Healing clears the pathway and helps you come home to your self and to your twin flame.

5. ABSENT HEALING AND PRAYER　　*TENDERNESS*

Absent healing and prayer for others will give you a link to the Divine, Angels and Guides. You can add this to your meditation at the end or sit for a few minutes in a special room, by a shrine or even whilst washing up. Send love and light to the person who needs your help and your angelic guides will do the rest of the work. You can simply ask Dr. Kruger and the team, to help, and they will be there in an instant. They are in service and are happy to help you and others.

6. BE POSITIVE　　　　*DIVINE PURPOSE*

Staying positive in all circumstances gets results. Take yourself lightly and laugh much of the time.

Negativity naturally pushes away opportunities and positivity automatically opens up all possibilities, thus bringing unexpected help to you. Using affirmations is always a good idea to let go of all struggles and release all blocks to abundance.

Once you are closer to soul you realise you are subtly transforming to become always joyful and balanced, then all worries disperse, as if they never existed.

AFFIRMATIONS
Choose one for each day and keep repeating it:

I am totally self honest
I do as I would be done by
I see God in everything
I am open and generous hearted
I stay calm and centred at all times
I detach from the third dimension
I take full responsibility for my life
I choose my friends and associates with care
I am aware of the Christ within
I accept everyone and everything as Divine
I work with Angels and Masters
I am the Violet Flame
I laugh a lot

VISUALISATION TO FIND YOUR SOUL PURPOSE AND MEET YOUR TWIN FLAME

1. Sit or lie in a comfortable and quiet place.
2. See yourself climbing a mountain. Take a few minutes walking up the windy paths, looking at nature around you.
3. As you near the top of the mountain breathe in the fresh air.
4. You then see twelve steps leading to the very top.
5. Each step has a colour, and each step you take, you feel more and more unconditional love. Climb each step very slowly and absorb firstly the Red; then Orange; Yellow; Green; Turquoise; Indigo; Violet; Aquamarine; Magenta; Gold; Peach; and finally Opalescence.
6. At the top of the mountain you see someone you know very well, but perhaps have forgotten. Everything about them is so familiar. The

way they behave, their speech, their looks, and what hits you the most is their incredible love for you. This is your twin who mirrors every aspect of your soul and knows you even better than yourself.

7. Embrace and feel and hear that which you need.
8. Ask the twin about your soul mission at this point in time and listen for the answer.
9. Ask to be shown how to achieve your mission.
10. Ask that the right people for your earth mission who are to help you, will become known to you.
11. Know that your twin is your Beloved, supports you constantly, and can never leave you. Promise to keep the doorway of connection open and ask that your twin remain, becoming more and more tangible in your consciousness.
12. Say thank you and know you can always return to the top of the mountain when you need to.
13. Open your eyes when you are ready.

7. BE IN SERVICE — *HUMILITY*

Being sincerely in service is not just beneficial to the receiver, but it gives you a sense of fulfillment and places you in trust with the Universe. It aligns you to the Supreme, to becoming unconditional and non-judgmental, thus lighting you up from within.

Offer yourself to be in service to the Supreme, and ask to work with great Love, always listening to your heart to guide you.

EXAMPLE
Make a list of all the things you did for others last week.
Make a list of all the things, however small or large, that you can do to help others for this week.
Make a list every week of your positive intentions for yourself and others.

8. COMMUNE WITH THE ANGELS   *FAITH*

Just call an angel to help with any task, from the mundane to the most glorious, and they will come. Pick an angel card to see which angel you are working with that day. Become accustomed to their qualities and absorb them to be more prominent in your life.

If you are a healer, ask an angel of a particular quality to work with you for your client. You can learn about the Essenes and their communions with various angels each day. Ask the angels to work with you in joy and laughter and watch your life change for the better.

VISUALISATION TO MEET THE ANGELS

1. Imagine yourself lying or sitting in a quiet place and close your eyes.
2. See a ball of gold above your head and allow this golden light to pour through your crown, right down to the base of your spine.
3. See the golden light pour through to each chakra spinning in front and back of the body. Firstly, the base chakra, spinning in front and back of the base of the spine. Then slowly pour the gold into the abdomen chakra, solar plexus, heart chakra, throat chakra, third eye and above the crown.
4. You are now placed in a golden light. The golden ray is the ray of the angels. Your golden radiance is resonating to their vibration.
5. The angels represent many qualities, such as joy, freedom, strength, openness, honesty, truth, peace, love, balance, beauty, forgiveness, and gratitude.
6. Call the angels to you and as you see them enter ask for three angels with the qualities you desire the most for the day.
7. Then, one by one, greet them and become each one. Absorb the qualities of these particular angels.
8. Thank the three angels for coming. Know that their qualities will now reside in your subconscious mind, to be shown in your conscious daily living.

9. Stay with the angels for as long as you wish. Have faith they are with you always and will help you in every situation.
Open your eyes when you are ready.

9. INTEGRITY   *TRUTH*

When you use your intuition, you will know who will be a compassionate spiritual teacher, therapist or friend. Without discernment, you can easily fall into many traps of the human ego. When involved in relationships and friendships, become lovingly detached. Keep high standards and discipline in all aspects of your life. Do not get involved with the third dimensional trappings and thinking, and stay in your own power.

Soul is our reality and is forever. All else is transient…

10. FROM YOUR HEART   *DIVINE COMPASSION*

Your heart leads you to your true soul awareness. Keep your heart open with unconditional love for self, as well as for others. Forgive and accept all in every circumstance. The heart chakra is the most important centre to work with when healing. The heart is where wisdom lies.

VISUALISATION FOR THE HEART CENTRE
The Rose

Imagine you are a rose bush—think of the roots, the stem, the leaves, and on top, one perfect rose bud. The rose bud is enclosed and enveloped by its green sepals—really take your time to visualise the details very clearly. Now imagine that the sepals are beginning to open, to turn back, revealing the delicate petals inside. Look at the colour—be aware of how perfectly formed the rosebud is, then the petals themselves slowly begin to open. As they do so, become aware and allow a blossoming to occur in the depths of your being.

Allow yourself to feel that something new is opening and coming to light just like the rosebud. As you continue visualising the rose, you begin to feel that its rhythm is your rhythm, and its opening is your opening. You keep watching the rose as it opens up to the light and to the air, as it reveals itself now in all its beauty.

You can smell its perfume, and you can absorb it into your being. Gaze into the very centre of the rose where its life is most intense, and let an image emerge in the centre. This image will represent the most beautiful, most meaningful, and most creative energy that wants to come to light in your life right now. It can be an image of absolutely anything. Just allow it to emerge spontaneously, without forcing or thinking. Stay with this image for some time, and absorb its qualities.

The image may have a message for you, a verbal or a non-verbal message. Be receptive to it. Place the rose into the very centre of your heart chakra, and open it up just like a rosebud. Each petal opens up to more and more Love and your heart is bursting forth wishing to share unconditionally.

11. BE CREATIVE   *BEAUTY*

Find one of your gifts, whether it is music, poetry, dance, art, colour, sound, or design. When you share your gifts, you are fulfilling your dreams. Your desire is to bring back beauty and magic, and light up the world. Creativity allows you self-expression; self-expression allows you freedom; freedom allows you to go Home.

VISUALISATION FOR BEAUTY

Close your eyes in a peaceful place.

Imagine that you are on a journey to find beauty. You begin in a place where nothing of beauty can be seen. Everything is stark and drab; the trees are bare, and the grass and sky are merely varying shades of grey. It is as if you are seeing the world as a black and white photograph.

The environment reflects the state of your spirit; you feel dispirited, as devoid of colour as are your surroundings.

Before you lay a grey path that seems to disappear into a mist. A great being of Love and Beauty appears and invites you to travel this path with him or her. Together you set out into the gloomy unknown. Gradually, the colour yellow comes into view. You notice patches of sunlight on the grey land. Dandelions appear on the grey grass, along with daffodils, buttercups, sunflowers, and daisies, all with their sunlit centres. Your mental energy is sparked by the introduction of the colour yellow. Even though the scenery is still bleak, you feel a spark of joy and hope, and are spurred on to continue along the road.

Now blue appears, colouring the sky, and joining with the yellow to bring the grass and trees to life. You feel the peace of the blue light and the healing energy of the green rays, which set off a green light in your mind. You want to go on, to proceed further and to learn more. You can feel your soul come alive within you. Beauty is beginning to enter your being, and your life.

The sky is suddenly glowing with the red, pink, orange, and purple hues of the sunrise. The bark of the trees and the earth emerge as reddish brown. The early morning shadows are a deep indigo. Flowers of all colours spring up everywhere.

You feel full of creative energy, enthusiasm, and connectedness to the magic of life. You realise the vastly important role that beauty plays in making you feel alive. Because you have experienced the drabness of a colourless world, you are now filled with a much deeper appreciation of Beauty than you have ever before experienced.

The being of Love and Beauty leads you to look up to the sky. You look up to see a wonderful rainbow arching from one end of the earth to the other. All the colours of the spectrum inspire you; you feel the vibration of each one drawing you into the different realms of beauty that they represent. Every aspect of your life is touched by Beauty. You close your eyes and feel this Beauty pulsating within you. You then

sense and see the vibrations within your soul. You realise that true beauty goes beyond sight, that the response to beauty is a response of your soul to the gift of life.
When you open your eyes, all the colours of the rainbow have merged into a magnificent white-gold light, and you feel the power of divine Love as the ultimate extension of all the beauty on earth.
You return from this journey with a renewed sense and appreciation of beauty. Wherever there has been drabness or despair, you are now able to feel the first rays of colour and life. Allow the colours to slowly permeate any areas of your life that need reawakening and revitalising. Be creative in any form you choose to decorate your life. Leave your mark and create signposts by which all will recognise their own soul.

12. BECOME LOVE *UNCONDITIONAL LOVE*

Ask Love to show you how to Love. Share Love with all you meet. The best thing you could do for another is to show them their Light and their gifts. Tell them you believe in them. Bear Love, yet, be open to receive

LOVE
Cultivate tolerance and patience.
Make contact with the Christ love.
Rise above the personality to the divine heart, and that light flowing into you will bring you warmth.
Then you won't have the emotional highs which humans equate with love, but something superior; a light, a gentleness, a sweetness, a kindness without words, will then flow from you.
That is Divine Love.
When you find it difficult, or almost impossible to love an individual, what you must do is forget all the little human failings and weaknesses within them, which make it so difficult for you to love, and give your heart to the Supreme.

Let the Supreme live as an image in your heart, and you will be flooded with light. You will have no difficulty then in feeling an immense love.
Seek for harmony in your human relationships.
Love your fellow men and women, your fellow creatures.
Feel in your heart the gentleness of the Masters.
Love, and your whole body will be recreated.
It will shine with the light of heaven.

Afterword

TWIN FLAMES

Channelled by Jayne Chilkes as her higher aspect Azraella
February 2001

Beloved Children of the Light–it is I Azraella. I speak to you as an aspect of Lady Jayne–I am in the Higher, Angelic. I work alongside my Beloved Lord Azrael, and we have been together since the beginning of time. We were caretakers and still are of the Angelic Realms.

Dear Ones, once you were together as one whole force, male and female, but as you descended to more earthly existences, became separated and agreed with the Elders to do so. You went on a journey of your own, separate from your Beloved, and only maybe once or twice, came across your Beloved or even married your Beloved in a lifetime or two. But the plan was to lead lives separately, to bring Light separately to the World. Each of you have a certain mission; each very individual in that mission and as the lives progressed incarnation after incarnation, you found yourselves waivering, almost forgetting each other. Thus the darkness fell on many of us, many of you, and it took some lifetimes to clamber out of what you may term Hell to reach Heaven once more. And many of you are in your last incarnation and are about to or have met your Beloveds.

Your Beloveds may even be on the earth plane, yet when two personalities come together there can be still some friction even though you know you are true Twin Flames at Soul. So one and the other have to be at the same level of evolvement to truly resonate thus otherwise causing havoc in your emotional bodies so in some ways it is much purer and finer if one is on earth and the other in Soul. For the one in Soul already knows who she or he is in all their Aspects. For all their Aspects make up the One, and mirror each of the Beloveds aspects who remain on the earth, dimmed, from the memory, but are awakening to remember. Thus, the Beloved in Soul draws them forward to remembrance. So eventually you regain your sight, your bearings, and you regain your continued centredness and feel more and more complete as your Twin beckons you forward, and in His or Her earthly incarnation that remains in Soul, closer to the earth than the higher vibrations of Soul, He or She can almost walk the earth with Thee.

Thus, being seen by thy side, you envisage their presence daily, having more and more intimate conversations; having more and more laughter, having more and more Light pouring through your entire being. Thus as the Light draws through you, it effects your physical body, and yes, it changes the structure, the infra-structure—the DNA of your physical body. Thus, your body can learn to be in the Light and as your body becomes more and more of the Light, you learn to disappear and reappear in an instant with thy Twins guidance. You are allowing thyself to travel the spiral of your being, of your souls essence to reach the Godhead. In the process of reaching the Godhead your inner souls' flame re-ignites and is seen by us and maybe by some in earthly embodiment. Your flame is activated above your crown reaching up to at least the top five chakras, above the crown reaching up to the Christed level and higher. And so you will regain clarity, you will regain divine purpose, joy and balance through your flame being re-ignited through your Crown upwards. For it is so used to being in the body traveling the earth doing mundane activities that are necessary while you are on the earth, it is forgetting during these mundane activities how to re-activate, until you take time to learn and feel your inner flame.

Dear Ones, you are on the verge of a great discovery. You are on the verge of discovering who you are. You are on the verge of knowing who you are in the many aspects that you conjure up from your soul. These aspects work with the many Soul Beings that are awake, working for God. You are resonating to Soul Families in the many realms that exist in Gods mansions, and you will find your Home wherebeit, and you will know your Twin when you find this Home.

You will find many teachers on the earth are being activated to this higher soul awareness, thus wherever you live or whatever part of the world you live, you will find a teacher who will regain your memory of your Twins existence. And even if your twin is on the earth plane, you can still readjust to his or her higher levels as you grow into yours, thus nothing is lost one way or the other—only to be gained; only Heaven on Earth to be gained. As you work with us in soul, you will remember that Angel part of thee, you will remember that Holy part of thee, you will remember the knowledge in one of your aspects, perhaps of Medicine, perhaps of Philosophy, perhaps of Science—whatever you care to remain in your Souls presences, will remain. You have the choice, but you do speak with the Elders to ask if these aspects are of sufficient benefit to the Soul family, and others who may need this information.

So dear ones, it is many levelled and very complex if you allow it to be so. I will not linger too much to explain the complexities of your Soul, but I will linger on sharing the Love of your Soul. For the Love of your Soul, especially blended with your Beloved, is beyond human dreams, is beyond human language. For as Twins, we are made from the essence of God, who for the most part is unfathomable in His/Her Love, and so are you! For it is Eternal. You will be learning new and great wisdom eternally. You will be free as Twins to go as you desire; to other galaxies, other planets, to understand all forms of being, all forms of light, all forms of intelligence, all forms of emotion, based on Love. For Love is infinite, Love is beauty, Love is precious, Love is All!

For when Love truly ignites its inner flame to its highest point, and Love penetrates your subconscious mind into the body's awareness into the lower chakras of the physical, you are ignited for this lifetime to travel in Light, in Love and in Service to the Supreme. When you feel this Love, you will know, and you will know the Presence of your Beloved through this Love.

Call your Beloved daily, every hour if you wish, for this gives Him/Her permission to step through, for they do not want to come if you do not want their presence. It is all finely monitored, so that you are not pushed in a hurry too forward, and you take each step very slowly, subtly and gradually. Dear Ones, you are totally protected in this procedure, for at this level there is nothing more than Love, Light and Support from the Elders, from the Masters, from God, from the Solar Logos, from all that have lived forever at this level and have watched over thee. You are protected and you are deeply loved and you are being drawn to where you belong. And that is Home with a capital H!

I thee Love with all my Heart and all my being and I greet thee and. Thank you for listening to my words on Twin Flames.

Azraella.

About the Author

Jayne Chilkes has been a Healer for over twenty years. She began her career as a fashion designer in London, being seen around town with Boy George, Spandau Ballet, and others in the famous "Blitz Kids" crowd. She was photographed, and also written about in all the leading magazines and newspapers. She then gradually decided to leave the fashion world, and dedicate her life to the spiritual path. She recently spoke about her Healing Work on TV, and starred as an Angel Expert on the Russell Grant Radio Show on Radio London.

She currently works primarily as a Channel of Soul Wisdom, and lives in the USA with her spiritual husband, whom she magically met on the Internet.

For appointments for:
Soul Channelling, Past Life Therapy, Hypnotherapy, Indian Head Relaxation Technique, Chakra Healing, Reiki, or Astrology Charts in the USA and UK
Please call 716 458-8844 or email: angels3@rochester.rr.com.

For information about forthcoming Angel Days, Indian Head Relaxation Technique, and Chakra Healing Courses in the USA and UK
Please call 716 458-8844, or visit Jayne's website at:
http://theangelschannel.netfirms.com.

Printed in Great Britain
by Amazon